FROM THE STREETS
TO A
MILLIONAIRE

HOW TO TURN ADVERSITY INTO MASSIVE SUCCESS

JASON GROSSMAN

Copyright © 2015 Jason Grossman

ISBN: 978-1-925341-07-2

Published by Vivid Publishing
P.O. Box 948, Fremantle
Western Australia 6959
www.vividpublishing.com.au

Cataloguing-in-Publication data is available from the National Library of Australia

CONTENTS

AUTHOR'S PREFACE

In this book you will read the true story of how the author went from dropping out of high school, being kicked out of home and living on the streets as a heroin addict, to not only becoming a millionaire but also creating a dream life that allows him to travel the world non-stop and help thousands of people across the globe.

Also in this unique book you will discover the powerful stories of many others who have looked into the eyes of death, illness, tragedy, hopelessness, homelessness, drug abuse, cancer, depression and other painful experiences of adversity that have raised up when all seemed lost, to not only overcome their adversity but to beat all odds and become incredibly successful and fulfilled in the process.

By reading this entire book you too can learn the secrets of how thousands of men and women before you, including the author, have faced their demons and experienced incredible pain in their life yet tenaciously created their definition of a dream lifestyle and incredible success. Wealth, health, happiness, freedom and true fulfilment are the desires of many, however not many will ever experience these feelings of abundance in the long-term, as they are consumed by their adversity, fear and grief rather than facing their fears and using it as motivation to be and do something phenomenal.

You have greatness within you, whether you see it yet or not, you are special, and regardless of your current circumstances, you do have the potential to do and achieve anything your heart desires and this book can inspire you and show you exactly how you can become the person you desire to, and are destined to be. As you read through this book and hang onto every word in anticipation, you will find the answers you seek, as a simple, pragmatic philosophy even a child could follow. Many people who read this book will do so with great interest, and yet will not act upon their findings. In fact, many people will start to read this book, but never finish it. Will that be you?

If you are reading this book, then congratulations, as there are people who have come to have this book in their possession and never even turned to this very preface. If you are reading this book, I'm guessing that it is because you want something more. Something more from life? To travel? To have more freedom? To create financial freedom? To create more deeply connected relationships? Or to become even healthier with more energy? It's only natural as human beings to desire more, but more doesn't always make us happy. In this book, you will discover how thousands of people before you have created abundance in their finances, relationships, health and wellbeing in order to live a dream lifestyle and achieve true fulfilment because success without fulfilment is truly failure.

This is not a get rich scheme or money making book. This book has one intention, and that is to inspire you with its true stories so that you can see that it is possible, whilst giving you the tools and resources to allow you to create your definition of a dream lifestyle that leads to true fulfilment. The journey is different for everyone. It means something different for everybody. Each new journey starts with a first step, and if you are prepared to take this first step with the author, you can begin to unlock the true potential of the unlimited reservoir deep within you, and transform your life forever.

This book is very unique as within many of the chapters, not only will you find written content with the why, what and how. You will also find the lessons the author has experienced on his personal journey of mistakes, stories of real life people, quotes to keep you going and most importantly interactive exercises. Thinking is not enough, you must act, and if you choose to act upon the exercises in this book you will quantum leap your results and fast track your dream lifestyle by years.

This book contains many experiential learning exercises that are referred to as home play. If you are serious about creating your dream lifestyle and achieving your definition of success, these exercises are highly recommended. However, I understand that many people won't. If you do choose to complete them, it will catapult your success rate, giving you a quantum leap forward by up to 12 months in how fast you will achieve massive success through the tools and resources you will uncover within this book.

To use this book and action the items effectively for maximum success, simply start with the first chapter, then complete the exercises then move on to the next chapter until all are completed. You may be thinking, well I just want to read the information and absorb it first, and that's fine, it's important you read this book the way you want. If all you do is simply read the entire book and action the lessons in everyday life you will still progress very quickly. If you truly want to create your dream lifestyle though I suggest taking one week on each chapter to read it, absorb it, and imprint it unconsciously and complete the exercises. Or if you prefer, read through the entire book first, then come back and spend up to a week on each of the chapters, completing the exercises.

Within this book, there are stories, some you may have even heard before. There are quotes and there are tools to use that you may have heard or seen before. I believe that we have the privilege, honour and responsibility to ensure some of the legendary learning's from the greats are passed down from these giants that have helped me and countless others turn adversity into success. I share some of these out of respect, as without them I would not be where I am today. However there are also many new stories, new information, new exercises and new tools that will be new to you, that you can easily apply in your everyday day life as well. This book is a manual of everything that I have personally learned and utilised, and continue to use, to get me where I am today. I now share this with you in the hopes that you too will find it inspiring and provocative in getting through the tough times and creating your dream lifestyle with true fulfilment.

For the reader that chooses to read this entire book from front to back with an open mind, absorb all the information like a sponge and apply the philosophies within, you will find yourself increasing your wealth and abundance in your financial world, health, relationships, mindset and personal self. Mediocrity is not a comparison to someone else, mediocrity is when we settle for anything in our life, in any of these realms, that is anything less than we deserve or are capable of achieving. This book invites you and challenges you to unleash the untouched infinite reservoir of unlimited potential within you and create true abundance in all these areas living a dream life with true fulfilment. Those that read and apply this book's contents will undoubtedly experience this on their incredible journey and adventure of life, almost immediately.

Finally, as we get ready to embark upon this journey together as two kindred spirits, remember there is a difference between knowing and doing. Can you truly know something without doing it? How hungry are you? How badly do you want to succeed? If you are ready to take the first step, leave where you are behind, and achieve greatness, now is the time to do it. Let's step up into your greatness together and take the first step now! Dream it. Believe it. Do it!

THE AUTHOR: Jason Grossman

ACKNOWLEDGEMENTS

As the quote by Isaac Newton goes: "If I have seen further than others it is because I stand on the shoulders of giants" and I would not be here, or have gotten through the tough times without the following giants. A huge thank you to all and everyone on my journey who have inspired me and kept me accountable, without the influence of each of you I would not be where I am today. Although literally hundreds have inspired me on my journey, the names that have had the most profound impact are as follows. In no particular order here are the people that have inspired me on my journey and in writing this book:

- Richard Branson
- Tony Robbins
- Jim Rohn
- Nelson Mandela
- T. Harv Eker
- Les Brown
- Zig Ziglar
- Dwayne (The Rock) Johnson
- Arnold Schwarzenegger
- Stephen Covey
- Napoleon Hill
- Stephen Hawking
- Brad Sugars
- Wallace Wattles
- Robert Kiyosaki

- Brian Tracy
- Wayne Dyer
- Deepak Chopra
- Eckhart Tolle
- Muhammad Ali
- Nick Vujicic
- Will Smith
- Will I Am (William Adams)
- Ellen Degeneres
- Eminem (Marshall Mathers)

Thank you again, words cannot describe how grateful I am to have had each and every one of you in my life on some level. Even though I haven't had the pleasure of meeting all of you yet, in time I hope and pray that I do, so I have the opportunity to shake your hand, or hug you, look into your eyes and say a deep and genuine, thank you from the bottom of my heart.

I would also like to personally thank the following people who without this book would probably not even exist.

My mum: I hope you can find it in your heart to forgive me for all the pain I put you through growing up; I knew no better. I literally wouldn't be alive today if not for you. I know we didn't always see eye to eye but you did the best you could as a single mum with kids. I blamed you for so many things growing up and I now know that it was always my doing through my own choices and my own actions. I'm so sorry for all the pain I caused and hope you can forgive me especially for some of the mistakes I made as a teenager and the way I hurt you in those years in which I share throughout this book. Thank you for doing the best you could at the time, I will always love you and have a special place for you in my heart no matter how far away from each other we are geographically.

My dad: Although we never really saw each other much growing up, you've always been there for me when I needed you. Whenever I needed you, you were always there. There were times especially as a teenager and young adult when I didn't treat you very well or show my appreciation, and for that I'm sorry. It took me years to forgive you for not being there when I was growing up, but I know the past is the past and although I've never heard you speak the words "I love you son" I know deep in your heart you have infinite love for me and all the kids. Although you weren't there for me in the early days, you've always been there for me since, and for that I'm forever grateful. I have become the man I am today because of the lessons I've learnt from you about family. We have never really been incredibly close, but not a day goes by where I don't think of you and your love for your family, and although sometimes you have trouble showing it, we know how much you care. I hope you can forgive me for all the pain I caused you and Tanya and I hope you know how grateful I am for both of you and all you've done. I would not be the man I am today and doing what I'm doing without your influence. For that I'm forever grateful. I love you Dad, and always will. Thank you.

The team and community: I would like to take the time to say a huge thank you to my current inner-circle as I write this book. Beau Zorko, Joshua Haswell, Ben Clarke, Lachlan Longmire, Jae Martin, Geoff Brown, Jordan Schouten and our entire community. We are so blessed and honoured to have such amazing people in our community – a community of kind, genuine, generous people with incredible values and a desire to contribute. Thank you to each and every one of you for your patience and for putting up with me over the years and being the glue in the community making it possible for us to impact so many lives. Without you the mission wouldn't be possible. Thank you so much to each of you for inspiring me to be the best I can and write this book. I never would have dreamed we would have created something so amazing that impacts so many lives and without you it wouldn't be possible. Thank you again to all the team leaders and entire community for being a part of something so magical.

My sweetheart: Thank you to my sweetheart Kailey, who literally saved my life. When things seemed so hopeless and I hit rock bottom you were there, you picked me back up. You lifted my spirits and raised me higher. You inspire me to become a better person, you challenge me to stay congruent to my values and keep me accountable to following through on my promises. You are the strongest, most patient, amazing person I've ever known. Thank you for always being there for me. Your love is a beacon, a guiding light leading the way for us to travel through this world helping people, changing lives and making a difference. Your kindness and strong values keep me going every day. You are the most special person I've ever known, I could not have done any of this without you. You are and always will be my rock, my girl, my world!

Some days seem dark, pitch black to no end.
Some days seem hopeless, and unable to mend.
Life can be a heavy burden, a weight slowing you down.
In a dark tunnel, with your feet stuck in the ground.

You can feel stuck hopelessly, unable to move.
It can feel pointless & useless, if you let in that mood.
Denied and shut down every corner and turn
You open your heart and others make it burn.

The pain of life, is a part of life's essence,
Pleasure exists not, in the absence of pains presence.
Light cannot exist without the grim dark,
That light starts within you, a light you must spark.

In times of adversity and pain remember,
you have the power to ignite that ember.
Stand tall, smile and choose today,
To light that spark, so you can see your way.

Jason Grossman

1

FROM THE STREETS TO A MILLIONAIRE

Your story can be either a fairy tale or hell on earth, choose wisely
as this fate will set you free or imprison you for life.

— Jason Grossman

When I was a young child, my mother and father who were quite young themselves, separated and got divorced. I don't remember the ordeal, but I do remember not long after when Mum remarried a man who was violent towards her on a regular basis. Soon they too were divorced, and after he set a bonfire and burnt everything, including pretty much all of my baby and child photos (I have only half a dozen now), we moved into a women's refuge to go into hiding. I was now the man of the house, just a child and the eldest of four.

Around that time is a bit of a blur for me I'm guessing for obvious reasons, but after a bunch of physical ordeals and dramas we moved to a suburb called Lockridge in Western Australia. At the time it was the roughest suburb in Western Australia, full of government housing, flats and units. I was quite a chubby kid who didn't seem to fit in and got picked on a lot because of it, so I became a bully. I remember getting into fights almost daily, including an ordeal with scissors.

Before too long I was in high school and that's when the fun began. The very first week at our school (the roughest in Western Australia), there was another kid that got stabbed repeatedly. It wasn't long before I was going to parties and smoking marijuana and drinking alcohol. We used to even go to buy casks of wine and smoke joints on our lunch breaks. We would even drink the casks of wine at the back of the class in school.

By year ten it was the norm to carry a knife for protection as there were fights most days and stabbings were common occurrences, and I even recall a few shootings. I was stabbed, hit in the back of the head with a sledgehammer and hit in the face with the back of an axe, all before the age of 16 when I was kicked out of home. That was when my mum told me that she was dying of cancer and we found out that she had really severe bipolar disorder. Now I was a homeless, a high school dropout.

Once I got kicked out I started staying at different friends' houses until I outstayed my welcome and my next option was youth hostels. That was when I started getting into more serious drugs including, Rohypnol, pills, speed and ecstasy. Within six months due to many issues I had caused within the hostels, I was banned from every hostel in Perth and had nowhere to stay but the streets, parks and any other place I could find in Perth where I wouldn't get arrested. I literally only had the clothes on my back and sometimes would go for days without food. I would beg for money but would spend it on alcohol. After six months on the streets I was introduced to heroin, and over the next 12 months is when I would get a real wake-up call. I now had a new circle of friends and they were all heroin addicts. I remember some days shooting up $1000 worth of heroin and I am sure you can guess where the money came from. That year I had many friends die from overdoses and car accidents, as well as being in a severe car accident myself plus getting hit by a car.

By that stage I had been arrested or locked up around a dozen times for a myriad of things and had overdosed twice. The third time I overdosed I died for a moment and they thought they had lost me and I knew that was the last straw and that I would end up dead or in prison if I didn't turn my life around. Once released from hospital I had absolutely nowhere to stay, so I rang my mum (who was in her third marriage), to clean up and detox. The first day wasn't so bad, the second was hard and by the third I was shaking in cold sweats and delusional (what you see in the movies is no exaggeration). I managed to get a few temazepam (valium) from my mum to help, but then ended up stealing the entire bottle and taking all fifty of them. I then went a little ballistic with an axe on the street (not knowing what I was doing), chopping at anything in sight. My mum's husband had threatened to shoot me, as he used to hunt, and I remember running straight for them at the door with the axe as they went inside. I went to start chopping at the door when I turned to the left and saw my sister with her face pressed against the window, fearful and in tears.

I came to, dropped the axe and fell to my knees crying – and I had never cried so much in my life – until the police came and I spent three nights in lock up, which forced me to detox. I had three whole days in solitude to think about my life. I was sad, then angry. I always felt from a young age that I was meant to do great things, that I was special, that I could make a difference in this world by leaving a legacy, but I had been doing the opposite. After that I committed myself and set my mind to being the best I could be and to giving back to society, and we all know that it takes time to really shift one's character, personality, habits and beliefs at the unconscious level.

Once I was released I spent a few days on a park bench with a pen and paper creating my plan. I was going to find a shared place to live, get a job and get into martial arts. So within a month of detoxing I had done all of these things. Just four weeks before this I was at a crossroads, to die, go to prison or fight for what I knew I could be. Do and have. It was hard but I began spending a lot of my time with martial arts and reading books about psychology to understand how the mind works. There were several relapses over the year but nothing too serious. I decided to do my personal training course and then got a job. Within nine months I was the busiest personal trainer in Western Australia and one of the busiest in Australia.

Exercise for the body (martial arts and the gym) and exercise for the mind (reading, courses and personal development seminars), was the key to my original success. People quite often ask me what my secret is, and there is no secret. I was just able to do something many say they can't do, which was to dissociate from all the people who had kept me in that life, which means that I had no friends anymore and also didn't see some of my family.

After doing PT my learning obsession grew and I studied business, and it wasn't until I came across NLP (Neuro-Linguistic Programming) and the therapeutic patterns that I was truly able to overcome my demons. I was ashamed and couldn't talk about my past, so I found youth and people I could share my story with in the hopes to inspire them, plus used NLP to overcome my demons; which I can gladly say I have.

After nine years of PT and other health and wellness businesses, I realised it was time for me to step up, so I started coaching Personal Trainers to grow their own businesses (my passions were business, health and fitness so it made sense). Next thing I know we were operating a seven-figure Health and Fitness Company with 17 amazing staff members helping to change lives worldwide through nutrition, coaching, health education, personal training and more, including working with charity organisations to make a difference and creating a million dollar business.

Growing a large business and truly making a difference (granted we had a long way to go), can be hard work, as you need resilience, intestinal fortitude, patience and the ability to overcome adversity. If it wasn't for my past experiences I truly believe that I wouldn't be doing what I am.

BUT THEN ... I went and did something crazy early in 2012, I fell madly in love with my sweetheart Kailey, the woman of my dreams. Next thing I knew I was closing down my company, and gave all my belongings away to my family and charity. I then moved from Perth to Brisbane (West Coast to East Coast) Australia to be with her. All with just a suitcase, $200,000 debt and an income of $297 a week.

I decided this time I wanted to set up a business that not only creates the healthy happy lifestyle for others anywhere in the world, but also allows me to live mine. I had built a seven-figure business in 18 months before, so surely I could do it again.

So this time in just nine months I built a seven-figure business completely online from scratch. Two and a half years later we have a team of almost 70 from across the globe helping people create happier, healthier lifestyles through nutrition, fitness, mindset, lifestyle design, financial freedom, charity and more. With online personal training, business coaching, life coaching, lifestyle design and a bunch of amazing programs, products and services to take one step closer to achieving our mission to help create one million happier and healthier lives!

Kailey and I have been traveling the world for some time now, and have had the amazing opportunity to visit 12 countries in just the past 12 months and now wherever we are we can run our online businesses, do live events and change lives, living our dream life through lifestyle design!

Helping people turn their dreams into reality is my true passion, as corny as it sounds, because it is possible if you make the choice.

The thing I'm most excited about this year is that Kailey and I will be launching our very own charity organisation, Youth of the World, where we will work with fundraising initiatives and events across the globe to assist youth with education, housing, health, career, lifestyle, drug abuse and much more.

I share this not to impress you but to impress upon you, so that you can see that no matter who you are, where you come from or what adversity you face, it's not how hard you get hit, but how you get up with a vengeance. And in the words of Eminem, "to not give up and not be a quitter" because you are special, and you can do great things. You have an untapped abundant reservoir of potential that once you tap into will surprise even yourself.

You can do anything, but you must do it now! The only way to fail is to quit; keep going and NEVER give up!

The first step to getting anywhere is deciding you are no longer willing to stay where you are.

—Unknown

WHERE DID YOU COME FROM?

Where did you come from? What is your story? We all have a story, whether it be sickness, death, a broken heart, financial crisis, homelessness, drugs, violence, alcohol abuse, or family issues.

The first step in beginning to create a dream lifestyle is to truly know and understand where you came from, appreciate it and accept that it's your past and you cannot change it. We can use the past to imprison ourselves with fear, or use it to learn about ourselves and unleash our full potential for true fulfilment.

In the beginning I was ashamed, I didn't want to share my story, and I hadn't drawn the lessons from my adversity. I know you have faced adversity. I know it's tough. I'm here to tell you, you can get through it. BUT you cannot drive forward if you are constantly looking in your rear vision mirror; sooner or later you will crash into a tree.

I found the best way to deal with my demons was to share my story to help inspire others, people like you. If you use it for motivation and inspiration for others, you can focus on what you can control, which is what you can give and the value you can add to others' lives.

I'm not an expert or better than anyone else, I'm simply a guy with a story to share with the world in the hope of easing the pain of some, inspiring others and helping many achieve their full potential in life. Sometimes all it takes is for the right person to come along and say: yes you might be content or even happy, but are you truly fulfilled? If you were brutally honest with yourself, what's not perfect about your life? What would you change or improve? Your health? Your relationships? Your finances? The lack of balance in your life?

Remember that the only way you can begin to move forward on this journey to creating your dream lifestyle is to unleash all of your demons, and then tame them, or they will hold you back.

Finally, remember the quote by Jordan Belfort, "The only thing standing between you and your goal is the bullshit story you keep telling yourself as to why you can't achieve it."

Will you let your story keep you in chains, or will you break free from those shackles and be liberated? Go out today and share your story and inspire someone to help them through. If you don't feel confident, speak to someone or people you don't know. But get started today!

Remember your dreams are as hungry as your demons.
Make sure you are feeding the right ones!

—Unknown

Deciding to close down my business in Western Australia to be with the girl of my dreams was an incredibly tough decision, however I chose to follow my heart. I chose love. It's not easy to close down a seven-figure company in a matter of weeks. I had to fire staff, break our lease agreement and get into over $200,000 debt and make some very tough decisions, but I knew deep down I was doing the right thing for us and for our future.

In the final two weeks leading up to the move from Western Australia to the East Coast I had nowhere to live so I had to sleep in the office, hoping the landlord wouldn't discover my secret. I would spend hours each night on the phone speaking to Kailey to help me through and remind me why I was doing what I was doing. In fact the last 48 hours before moving over to be with her I couldn't even afford to buy food and went several days with nothing but water. Remember this was only two and a half years before writing this book. At one stage I didn't even have access to a toilet and I had to pee in a bucket.

I had become a workaholic and subordinated my health, friends, family and romantic life for the success of the business, and now I was giving it all up, for love.

When I first arrived in Brisbane I had lost a lot of weight and was diagnosed with glandular fever. I would spend days on end in bed with barely enough energy to go to the toilet. I had made big promises to Kailey and didn't want to let her down, so I pretty much spent six months working on my laptop from the bed just to deliver on those promises. I felt so depressed some days I just wanted to quit. Everything seemed pointless, there were even times when I questioned whether life was worth living. I remember thinking how tough it was, and how hard it was to motivate myself to deliver on my promises. I had risked it all, I was all in and I was out of options, I had no choice but to succeed.

I understand as you read this that you are right, I don't know you or where you came from, or what you have been through. I understand things can get tough, very tough. But I do know that we all have a choice and that includes you. You can choose to do something about it. No matter how tough it is for you right now, ask yourself, in 12 months from now will this really matter? What can I do to fix this or solve the problem? No matter what you are going through right now this too shall pass and you can make it through. There is light at the end of the tunnel.

Sometimes we do get ourselves caught between a rock and a hard place, but that doesn't mean we have to stay there, we are not a tree, if we don't like where we are we can move. A plant is a plant, it can never be anything more, a dog is just a dog it can never be more than a dog. But you – you can do, be and achieve anything. I'm living proof. The people in this book are living proof. But you must believe.

The first step is to decide you are no longer going to stay where you are. You are no longer going to settle for that life. You are no longer going to put up with it. You are no longer going to settle, you are going to raise your standards and leave it all behind you. Have you been living with the pain so long it's just become a part of your life? Become so disturbed that you cannot possibly stay in your current situation. Mediocrity is not a comparison to someone else, mediocrity is when you settle for a life that's anything less than you are capable of or deserve, but you must take that first step, you must take action now and decide that you will no longer use your story as an excuse. You can do something about it; you have the power to change your world.

Only when the pain of your current lifestyle becomes greater than the pain and uncertainty you will experience on your journey to creating a dream lifestyle and creating fulfilment, will you do something about it. After working with over 5000 people to assist them with weight loss and body transformation as a personal trainer I really noticed this to be true in overweight and obese people. Only when the pain of their current life becomes greater than the pain of the journey they must embark upon with nutrition, fitness and mindset to lose that weight, will they do whatever it takes to lose it. Unfortunately this is why many people have a heart attack then decide to lose weight or get healthy, and often it's too late. Will you leave it until it's too late? Will you wait until you have a proverbial heart attack?

What must you do to get really disturbed and create so much pain in your current life so that you will no longer accept it? If you are truly honest with yourself, what do you not like most about your life? What creates the most pain in your life? I know it seems harsh but it will be that pain that motivates you to not use the same old BS story that was keeping you from achieving your dreams and taking that first step today. Pain creates hunger and hunger motivates you to take action. Take action today and you can transform that pain into pleasure, happiness, joy and more importantly, fulfilment. You've got to be hungry. You've got to want it bad. How hungry are you?

Never forget your story, and remember where you came from, use it as a driving force to propel you forward with massive action and laser beam focus. Remember though, there is a difference between using your story as an excuse and using your story as motivation. One will keep you imprisoned in shackles the other will set you free and allow you to soar. Isn't it time you soared? Now is your time to soar. Now is your time to put the past behind you, create some urgency in your life, be hungry, stay hungry and take massive action.

Once you make the decision to move on, don't look back.
Your destiny will never be found in the rear view mirror!

—Mandy Hale

In taking the first step to achieving your dream lifestyle, not only do you need to stop using your old story as an excuse but you also need to forgive. You cannot drive forward if you are looking in the rear vision mirror all the time and expect not to sooner or later hit a tree. Forgiving yourself and others is an essential key to successfully taking that first step. We can't control others forgiving us, what we can control is forgiving ourselves and others. Until I was 28 I blamed my parents for a lot of the hardship and adversity I experienced. Then I realised it was all based on my own decisions. In fact if it wasn't for my mum and dad I wouldn't be here in the first place. Then I also realised that sometimes reverse role models are just as important as role models, and all the decisions they made that influenced my life were necessary for me to be the person I am today. It sounds a little clichéd but true, if I hadn't lived on the streets, been a heroin addict, been kicked out of home and a high school dropout, there is a good chance I would not be writing this book right now in the hope of inspiring people to live a happier, healthier life.

There is a great story I am reminded about with forgiveness and moving forward.

Two monks were walking through the forest. During the course of their journey, they came to a river where they met a beautiful woman – an exquisite creature, dressed in expensive clothes and with her hair done up classy. She was afraid of ruining her expensive clothes, so continued to ask the monks if they might carry her across the river.

The younger of the brothers was offended at the very notion and turned away with an attitude of disgust. The older brother didn't hesitate for a second, and swiftly picked the woman up on his shoulders, carried her across the river, then set her down on the other side. She thanked him and went on her way, and the monk waded back through the waters back to his brother.

The monks resumed walking, the older one peacefully, while the younger one grew more and more annoyed then angry. He then stopped his older brother and shouted, "Brother, we are taught to avoid contact with women, and there you were, not just touching a woman, but carrying her on your shoulders!"

The older monk looked at his younger brother with a loving

smile and said, "Brother, I set her down on the other side of the river; you are still carrying her."

Who or what are you still carrying? Isn't it time you put them or it down? Imagine the weight that would be lifted from your shoulders, the feeling of freedom and liberation. Do you ever feel like you are carrying the weight of the world on your shoulders? Isn't it time you put that weight down? Give yourself permission and forgive yourself right now. Put the past in the past, let bygones be bygones and relieve yourself from that unnecessary pain that you chose to hold on to up until now. As you put that weight down, notice how that makes you feel. Feel the freedom and the lightness.

Remember you cannot move forward without hitting a tree if you are looking in the rear vision mirror, and the weight on your shoulders will just slow you down even more with gravity pulling you down on your journey to success. Let it go now, put the past behind you and let's take the next step together with a newfound sense of lightness in your step, energy about your walk and smile on your face. Who do you forgive right now?

When you forgive, you do not erase the memory. You simply choose to forgive to free yourself from bitterness. The memory stays, not to be forgotten but to be remembered as a valuable lesson.

—Unknown

2

MANIFEST AND INTENSIFY YOUR WHY

The fuel for the fire that motivates us to jump out of bed every morning and take massive action, build unstoppable momentum and transform our dreams into reality is our WHY!

—Jason Grossman

Just weeks before my 16th birthday I came home stoned on pot during the day and my mum and I got into an argument. Now I'm really not proud of what happened next, but I want to invite you to remember this book isn't just about success it's also about mistakes and failure, and then learning from them and dealing with them. My mum slapped me and as an immediate reaction I pushed her back and she hit a wall and fell to the floor. I couldn't believe it. I ended up in tears. How could I do this? How could I let myself do something so terrible?

I could blame the drugs, and to a degree that explains some of the behaviour but it certainly doesn't justify it. That was the exact moment I was kicked out of home and left with just a backpack and some clothes. It took me years to forgive myself for that. I blamed my mum for my youth, I couldn't forgive myself for my erratic adolescent behaviour. Then as I grew a little older I realised it was up to me to forgive and move forward.

There was a time as a teen when I lived with my dad. I remember getting so angry with him that I threw a dumbbell at him and although I missed (thankfully) it was enough to cause a rift and create pain. Although before the age of 13 he wasn't there, my dad was and has always been there since I've been an adult. He has always gone out of his way to be loving and supportive and lend a hand when needed.

These are some huge mistakes that I know I had to forgive myself for, in order for me to grow as a person. You may judge me for them and for that I understand. What mistakes have you made though? What actions have you taken out of character for you that you haven't forgiven yourself for? Isn't it time you forgive yourself even if that person hasn't? You are right in that you cannot change the past, but you can change the meaning you give it. The only power you have is in the now, and now is the time to forgive and move on. That was the old you, the new you would never do that. Now it's time to know that, and prove that to yourself and the world. This doesn't mean that you won't make mistakes, it just means that you will learn from your old behaviour and become a better person because of those mistakes and your forgiveness.

My why burns so brightly it forms a magnificent obsession. Since I was a young child I've felt I was meant to do great things, I felt I was special. Did you ever feel like this as a kid? Did you ever feel like you were here for a reason? Ever felt you are special and meant to do something great? That's because you are. My motivation now is fuelled by the fact that I feel obliged to give back to the world as repentance for my mistakes and actions, which I take full responsibility for, and to help others get through their tough times. If possible to even help them avoid it in the first place. No child or youth should have to go through so much pain that it's almost unbearable to be alive. This is why I created the charity organisation Youth of the World. We assist youth ages 4-17 in getting off the streets, off drugs, out of violence and abuse. We also assist youth who are terminally ill and provide education for life skills. This is my biggest passion and my own experiences growing up were necessary to fuel the fire and motivate to give back on a large scale.

This will be my legacy to the world, a charity that forever more helps kids across the planet create a happier, healthier and safer life. What legacy will you leave? What is your why? What is your purpose? If you are unsure, start by following your passions and along the way you will find the answer.

When I do have children I want to be there and see the first step, hear the first words and ensure that they have a magical life even after I leave this world. I don't want them to ever have to experience all the pain I did growing up. Imagine, what a gift for the world, what a gift for your family. Don't you and your family deserve a magical life? If you help enough people get what they want, you will have everything you want. But it's got to be genuine and not solely for that reason. It's got to stem from your desire to help others and love others. What are you most passionate about? If you could leave this world a better place, how would you? How would you make a difference? It's possible!

So congratulations on making it to chapter two. If you are still reading hopefully that means you haven't judged me and my mistakes too harshly (and there have been many) and you are ready to put your past behind you. Once you know your story and are ready to commence your journey, before you take the next step you need to know what direction you are heading in, and more importantly, why you are heading there. If we don't know where we are heading, how can we arrive at where we wish to be? And if we don't know why we are heading there, we won't feel the necessary motivation to take the steps, especially on the tough days; you know, those tough days when life knocks you down? You don't have the energy, your partner left you, you are sick, a close family member leaves this world, or you can't even pay the bills.

When you know exactly why you are on this journey, you manifest it daily by thinking about it consciously morning and night, then intensify it until you become relentless in the pursuit of your dreams, and do whatever it takes, for as long as it takes, until you have achieved your dream lifestyle.

A massive part of my why is twofold. The first is that growing up we didn't have a lot, and I went through a lot of pain and much adversity in my youth and don't wish that upon anyone. I would love to inspire millions of people to get through such pain, or even to avoid it in the first place. Doing this, in a way I can leave a legacy for my family's future, which is also a huge motivator. Secondly, when I do have children I want to be there and hear their first words, and see their first steps, don't you?

Only when the pain of your current lifestyle becomes greater than the pain you will experience from the action you take to achieve it, will you do it. Become so disturbed with your current lifestyle, that you must make changes. What are you most disturbed about? What are you going to do about it?

Remember mediocrity is not a comparison to someone else, it is when you settle for a life that's anything less than you deserve and are capable of. Are you playing at 100%? Are you doing everything in your power to create abundance in your health, wealth and relationships? Have you settled or are you comfortable? Have you been in your comfort zone up until now? Billions of people are going to die not achieving their definition of a dream lifestyle let alone take the first step. Will you be one of them? Will you coast through life just surviving, or will you thrive? Isn't it time you thrived?

I believe you are special, you are different and have greatness within you. That's why you are reading this book, because I believe you are in the 2% that will do something about it, take action and achieve your heart's wildest desires – to live the life you were born to live.

Family can be an incredible motivator and a huge part of our why. I came across an article by Carla Adair Hendricks (*AARP Bulletin*, 2011) about Herbert and Zelmyra Fisher, married 86 years, who hold the Guinness World Record for the longest married couple. Herbert and Zelmyra have both since passed away but their story is nothing short of incredible and it continues to inspire.

The husband and wife from North Carolina were married in 1924 and built their family home in 1942, where they lived together up until the death of Herbert in 2011.

The Fishers didn't believe that there was a secret to the longevity of their marriage but that their religious beliefs played a big part.

Whether you believe in god or not, there is no denying that when you believe the purpose of something, it is that of divinity and a higher power – kind of like a calling – that empowers you with an incredible why and will to go on.

Herbert was an avid saver and a frugal spender and as a result was able to pay for all five of their children to go to college. They had ten grandchildren, nine great-grandchildren and four great-great grandchildren. WOW.

It was their granddaughter Iris Godette who was responsible for arranging the Guinness World Record recognition back in 2008 when they had been married for a whopping 86 years.

They had stayed together through wars, depressions, financial hardship and more, but they always worked as a team and believed that there was a way to keep their love and make it work.

What an incredibly inspiring couple. It reminds me of a saying I once heard another older couple say, "We have managed to stay together for so long because we were born in a time when something was broken we would fix it!" WOW, such empowering words. People and family can be such a powerful why. Who do you have in your life that inspires you to be the best that you can be? Who would you love to give a life of everything they ever dreamed of? A life they truly deserve? You deserve it. They deserve it. What are you waiting for? What are you prepared to do to make it happen? Do you know what drives you? What is your why?

You want to clarify your why, magnify it then intensify it. Transform your why into a magnificent obsession and use that as the driving force to get you through the hard times, the pain, the hardship and the adversity. Your why is what will propel you forward each and every day.

> *The purpose of life is to discover your gift.*
> *The meaning of life is to give your gift away.*
>
> —David Viscott

In Neuro-Linguistic Programming (NLP) there are conceptual filters known as Meta-Programs, these programs determine contextually how we filter our representation of reality. NLP believes that most behaviour is either motivated by moving towards pleasure or away from pain. Although it is a little deeper than that as it doesn't consider values, beliefs and other distinctions, it really is a great starting point to begin to understand what makes you tick.

Toward versus away motivation

It's 6pm in sunny Western Australia and in a comfortable little home resides a small family with a father cheerfully setting the table for dinner, mum cooking a delicious roast in the kitchen and a 12-month-old baby boy playing in his playpen. As the father sets the table, mum walks out to place a scrumptiously healthy salad on the table. Then somehow the baby boy manages to escape from his playpen and begins to crawl adventurously towards where there is an array of olfactory stimulating aromas oozing from the kitchen.

The baby boy then for the first time ever manages to grab hold of the oven door handle pulling himself to a complete upright position on his feet, and as he wobbles unsteadily back and forth, never having experienced a hot oven door before now, places his left hand with an open palm directly on the hot oven door. The baby boy lets out a scream which grabs the mother and father's attention and they rush post-haste to the kitchen, but not before the inquisitive infant then goes in for a second touch of the steaming hot door, falls to his knees in a heap crying loudly then turns the other way to crawl quickly away from the hot door and towards his mother.

Now besides the fact that you might be thinking, well a parent should never let that happen, let's be honest, babies, toddlers and kids in general get themselves into mischief; it seems to be part of life. But can you relate to this story in any other area of your life? Has there ever been a time when things may have been a little tight financially so you borrowed money, or got an extra job or took some kind of action to make more money. What about with your health and fitness or weight? Many people for whatever reason at some stage find themselves looking in the mirror or stepping on the scales and saying to themselves, "How did I let myself get like this?"

So what next? You join a gym, start walking or jogging and perhaps start a diet and tell yourself it will never happen again. You then lose some weight and achieve a body you are more comfortable with then next thing you know the amount of gym sessions shorten, treats start sneaking back in, alcohol consumption is increased again and so on.

This is what I refer to as our 'physical thermostat'. The worst possible shape we let ourselves get to before we do something about it. For athletes, it may be 10% body fat. A single mum might be 80kg on the scales. Many guys have a thermostat of 100kg, "Oh no three digits, time to go back to the gym!"

One of the main reasons for this yoyo behaviour is due to a meta-program or conceptual filter, which is a subconsciously habitual response to external stimuli known as Towards Vs Away motivation.

Much of what we do in life is to move towards pleasure or away from pain. When we are focused on moving towards our eyes are set firmly on the prize, the target and not obstacles, and we will do everything in our power to travel unequivocally towards the goal. When we are towards motivated our focus is on the end result and what we focus on expands and that is what motivates us. Our language is then also more congruent and we will not stop until it's attained. Getting a certain job, sporting achievements, academic achievements, the girl of your dreams, are all examples of towards motivation. Towards motivation is a powerful tool in being persistent to do whatever it takes to attain your goal and it is backed with flaming desire and strong beliefs and values to boot.

Away motivation however, just like the baby above, is when we focus on what we don't want, we are looking at what we don't want and moving away from it with our back towards our goals and not our eyes. Our eyes and focus are still fixed on the pain. As the baby touched the hot plate notice he felt pain but he only moved his hand far enough away to no longer experience that pain. The problem with away motivation is that this is what leads to inconsistencies in life, you focus on moving away from what you don't want but only far enough away so there is less pain. Can you relate this experience to any other area in your life?

This is why it can be easy to spiral to a point where we become overweight or even obese once the momentum starts because only when the pain of our current state of living becomes greater than the pain of the process of losing the weight will we act upon it. Plus with weight loss is it toward or away motivated? Are we focused on moving toward what we want or away from what we don't want? Away from what we don't want, right? Because we are thinking about the weight that we don't want, and so we are focusing on what we don't want, then we get more of what we don't want. Hence the inconsistencies and yoyo results. We need to take a leaf from the baby's booklet, turn around face the other way and move towards your goal. Even focusing on a specific weight on the scales, if focused on in a certain way, can have the adverse effect as you are focused on losing weight you think about weight and it becomes away motivated, you then only change your habits and actions long enough to move away from the pain then slip back into your old habits. But not anymore. Right!

This is also true with dieting. What's the focus with dieting? Food yeah, so guess what expands and you focus on more? How hungry you are or the foods you can't have or your favourite snacks until you cannot bear it and make excuses like, well I was good this morning, or I went to the gym today. I should do this and I tried to do that.

So as you can see, to empower yourself with the motivation and persistence required to achieve your goal long-term it's important to focus on 'towards' motivation. You ask, well that's great Jason but how do I do that? Well it's simple, it's our language, the way we speak to ourselves. Become aware of that little voice in your head (that never stops) and notice how you speak to yourself. For example, instead of saying, I'm going to lose 20kgs because I'm overweight, set a goal and use specific language to say, I'm going to achieve a healthy body weight of 60kgs because that means I will feel healthy and happy. Write it somewhere and read it out loud for five minutes a day. What other areas of your life can you notice this to be true?

One of the most profound and motivating movies I have ever

watched is *The Pursuit of Happyness*, have you seen it yet? If not I highly recommend it as it is a perfect example of what someone is capable of when their why is strong enough and becomes a magnificent obsession.

The movie is based on the true story of Chris Gardner and his incredible journey. It tells a story of a father who earned a spot in the Dean Witter Reynolds training program but became homeless when he could not make ends meet on his meagre trainee salary.

The movie shares how through Gardner's ferocity, focus and his strong why (his son) he persisted to turn his dream into a reality, even as a homeless man with his son sometimes sleeping in a public toilet because they had nowhere to stay. How Chris was able to turn that adversity into massive success is one of the most inspiring stories of going from the streets to a millionaire that I've ever seen.

Now not only has Chris become a multi-millionaire but now he also runs initiatives to help homeless people across the United States and presents to thousands of people to inspire them to live a happier life and turn their adversity into massive success.

We all have a story, and that story we tell ourselves will determine many of the choices we make in our life. What story do you still tell yourself?

In understanding what motivates us – pain or pleasure, towards or away orientated – It's important to understand that the most powerful motivating force to take the first step before there is any momentum is, pain. It's away motivation. Pain is what creates hunger and hunger creates drive, drive creates action and that action builds momentum. What was Chris's first motivation? Pain, right? The pain of living on the streets. The pain of seeing his son unhappy. However, he didn't continue to focus on that pain, did he? He then turned around and focused on one thing, his success, and he became toward motivated.

Unconsciously, many of us become disturbed by looking in the mirror or at our bank balance and that creates pain. So that pain creates hunger and we are motivated to take action. Now in our mind we know that it was the pain that motivated us to take the first step, the first action. So unconsciously we form the belief that pain is always the driving force. Makes sense, right? That's what made us take the first step. If you've only taken one step and it was driven by pain, you have nothing to compare it to, as it's the only step. It wasn't towards motivation that motivated you to take the first steps. Not for long-term success and fulfilment anyway.

So for long-term success and happiness, what do you want to use as your driving force for the second step and each step following?

If you continue to use pain as a motivator, you will still be focusing on what you don't want, so you will only move far enough away from what you don't want, until you feel less pain. After you take the first step you want to then turn the other way, as did the child from the hot stove, and focus on what you do want. By doing this you will be fixated on what you do want and you won't be distracted by other trivial problems, and with your strong why you will be pulled towards your happiness, success and your dream. Make sense?

So yes, use pain as the driving force to take the first step, but once you have put your story, the pain and your past behind you, turn around and now focus on what you do want and watch it expand, and notice how your dream will pull you towards it almost effortlessly.

It's kind of like a strongman. You know the strongman competitions where they have a harness strapped to their back and a rope attached from that harness to a truck? They get down nice and low and exert 100% of their energy just to take the first step and create some movement so that stationary truck will begin to move. That first step is the hardest. They then take another step, and another, building more and more momentum until they reach a point where they can easily and effortlessly walk past the finish line and the truck continues to role on past the finish line on its own wheels, even after they stop walking.

It's the same with your goals, your hopes and your dreams. The first step is the hardest. You need to use pain to take that first step to generate enough force to create movement. But once you do take that first step (your first action) and decide to no longer stay where you are, with EVERY step after that you need to then focus forward and look at the finish line with laser beam focus. As you stay focused on that finish line you will build the momentum and it will become even easier for you, until you simply walk across the finish line with ease and your dream becomes a reality.

My mission in life is not merely to survive, but to thrive; and to do so with some passion, some compassion, some humour and some style.

—Maya Angelor

One of many men that has personally inspired me with his story of being adopted at only six weeks old and facing stories of impossibilities as told from other people until he realised he could write his own story and create his own destiny, is motivational speaker Les Brown. Arguably one of the world's best speakers and a legend. I love listening to Les Brown, there's something about his voice that's comforting and soothing but his story is what really revs me up.

Les and his twin brother were adopted at only six weeks old by Mamie Brown, a single lady that was of humble financial background. As Les says though, with a very big heart. Les was labelled with a learning disability at school and faced a lot of hardship growing up and as a result he didn't continue any education after high school. Experiencing low self-esteem and other challenges, he faced his fears and demons to become a leader in the public speaking realm touching millions of hearts and inspiring people across the globe. The one liner that stuck with me most is found just below. If you've ever had a bad day, a tough day, a rough day, a day where life has knocked you down, I'm sure in time you will agree that Les is one of those go-to voices and people to get you through. He is the ultimate motivator and genuinely a kind and generous soul. His story continues to inspire me, and I highly recommend you take the time to attend one of his training sessions or purchase one of his audio programs.

Les's story really resonated with me personally. His struggles in school and the hardship he faced, and it lifted me up when I heard all he had done to face that adversity to accomplish greatness. You too as Les says have greatness within you and you are special; I agree!

One of his driving forces was his strong family values and the promises he made to his mum, a man that oozes integrity and tenacity surely was always destined to inspire millions. Thank you Les for all you do and continue to do.

When life knocks you down, try to land on your back. Because if you can look up, you can get up. Let your reasons get you back up.

—Les Brown

If you have tried hard, over and over just to fail and you feel like you are almost hitting your head against a brick wall perhaps it's your why (or lack of) that was holding you back. Maybe it was your BS story. When your why is strong enough, and you focus on it clearly enough you will persist until you are successful. Imagine the difference between being in a canoe paddling up the river versus being in a jet boat powering down the river. Not having a why is like paddling – working harder and harder for slower results, burning out, feeling fatigue and despair. If you become crystal clear on your why, manifest it at the unconscious through daily cultivation then intensify it through emotionalising your vision, it will always get you through those tough times.

Following these three crucial steps everyday are the key to motivating yourself to take massive action daily and form a magnificent obsession for the attainment and achievement of your dream lifestyle. When you follow these three simple steps everyday no matter how tough life gets, no matter how many times you get knocked down, your why and your reasons will get you back up.
1. Gain clarity on your why.
2. Manifest and cultivate your why.
3. Intensify your why.

The easiest way to determine your strongest and most compelling why is to simply ask yourself what is more important to me in my life than anything else? What do I value more in my life than anything else? Then all we need to do is link your number one value to your goal of creating a dream lifestyle and how exactly that goal can feed and nourish your number one value. Throughout this book we will talk about the power of beliefs, values, habits, goals and more. For now it's simply following these three steps before we go any deeper down the rabbit hole.

1. What is your why? _____
2. Manifest your why: By thinking about it as often as you can every day.
3. Intensify your why: By adding emotions to it by visualising having already achieved it, meaning looking through your own eyes.

Don't you want to create a dream life for you and your family? Don't you want to leave a legacy for them that they can pass down for generations? Don't you want to teach them anything is possible and values of integrity and abundance? Do they not deserve it? Even if you don't have a family yet, perhaps one day you will.

The mind doesn't recognise the difference between remembering the past, experiencing the present or imagining the future. And when you emotionalise through associating into your vision of having already achieved your why it will intensify immensely.

If you are serious about creating your dream lifestyle, take the time to write down the answers to the following questions with passion and enthusiasm, which will assist you in these three steps. I understand this can be a little difficult at first, but the more you do it, the easier it will become.

My definition of a dream lifestyle is: _____
_____

(Be sure to use sensory data terms such as 'looks like', 'sounds like', 'feels like' and more importantly word it in a way that you can show someone else you've achieved it and it's tangible)

Why is it so important for me to achieve my dream lifestyle? ____

_____

What will it really mean to me if I were to achieve my dream lifestyle? _____

_____

On a scale of 1-10, with 10 being the most, how important is it that I achieve my dream lifestyle?_____

_____

How would I feel when if in 6-12 months from now I'm still exactly where I am right now? (Remember to make it as painful as possible)

_____

_____

How will I feel if I take the necessary action and do achieve my dream lifestyle? (Remember to make it as pleasurable as possible)

_____

_____

If I keep doing what I have been doing up until now, am I guaranteed to achieve my dream lifestyle in the near future? Y/N _____

What am I going to do about it?_____

_____

If you can't figure out your purpose, figure out your passion. For your passion will lead you right into your purpose.

—Bishop T.D Jakes

Did you answer the previous questions? Even if you didn't write them down did you answer them in your head? These are your dreams we are talking about, don't you owe it to yourself?

Are you prepared to take time each day, each morning, each evening to cultivate and intensify your why until it becomes a burning desire imprinted eternally on the canvas that is your unconscious mind? To form a magnificent obsession that creates so much drive and motivation deep inside you that it feels like an unstoppable force no obstacle to stop?

Isn't it time to put that old story to rest then cultivate your why and intensify it? The only time you have any power to influence your future and shape your destiny is right now. Will you keep using the same old story that was holding you back until now from propelling yourself forward in life? Or will you forgive and learn? Will you keep looking in the rear vision mirror at what's behind you, or will you start focusing on the journey ahead?

Has there ever been a time you've stopped at a red light in your car and for a brief moment you check your phone, look down or get distracted and then you hear a 'HONK' of a horn beating from a car behind you, and you just put your foot on the gas and accelerate forward in response?

Have you ever set your alarm for tomorrow morning to be sure to awaken on time, then when it goes off and you hit snooze, it then goes off again, and maybe even a third time then you know that you have to get up now and get ready for the day? I've even found myself on the third snooze counting down the seconds, three, two, one okay time to get up, NOW!

Now is the time to put the past behind you where it belongs, today is a new start, the first day of the rest of your life. Start your day with intention, your why, your mission and begin to notice how things become a little easier and tend to go your way much more, and even when they don't you find yourself shrugging your shoulders and saying, "oh well".

What motivates you? What drives you to take action and get you out of bed every day? Use your why, your purpose and your motivation daily to jump out of bed like your bed is on fire and embrace the day with enthusiasm and gusto living each day as if it is your last, remember life is a gift and a gift is opened and truly enjoyed in the present.

It's time to truly live, it's time to step up and take the next step … now is your time to be phenomenal!

Cultivate, Manifest and intensify your why everyday and you will never have to be disciplined or have willpower again!

—Jason Grossman

3

CREATE YOUR DREAM LIFESTYLE

Dreams are like six pack abs, everyone wants them but only a few are prepared to do whatever it takes to have them!

—Jason Grossman

From the age of 14-20 there are literally weeks at a time of my life that I cannot remember. I remember now waking up one morning in a pool of blood with cuts and bruises and motor oil all over me. I realised I had been hit by a car and didn't even remember it having taken place. I have woken up in hospitals not knowing how I got there or why I was there. And this is just the beginning. I used to drink alcohol and take every drug under the sun to inhibit my perception of reality, which was distorted and filled with so much pain. Have you ever been there? In a dark place? Been in a hole? Like I did, you too can climb out of that hole and achieve incredible things in this life. This book offers you a ladder, as it did me, to climb out of that hole. We all have stories, and this book is about helping you turn your life around from wherever you are now to achieve massive success and create your definition of a dream lifestyle.

Your dreams are possible, regardless of where you are now economically, environmentally, relationally or health wise you can get through it and turn your dreams into a reality.

Would you like more clarity and certainty in your life? Would you like more direction? The key to having more certainty and clarity is to not only know your why, it's also having a plan for exactly what you want and how you are going to get there. This chapter is about doing exactly that – determining what you want to achieve in your dream lifestyle. Then creating a specific plan to make it a reality.

If you have a business and you wish it to be successful, do you not have a business plan? If you want to lose weight or become an athlete, do you not have a fitness and meal plan? I'm sure you would agree you want to have a plan for these achievements, so why don't you have a plan for your life yet?

There are many facets and ways to create a lifestyle design plan, and in this section we are going to start with the two most fun and exciting parts.

I believe life is about creating magical memories with loved ones, and a bucket list is a great way to have a plan to ensure you make the time to create those magical memories. A plan for all the things we normally put off and call important, but not urgent. Travelling, learning a language, learning to play an instrument, climbing Mount Everest, meeting a mentor or celebrity, or competing in a challenge like an iron man or triathlon event.

A bucket list is also a great way to keep yourself accountable and to stop living groundhog day. Do you ever feel like today was the same as yesterday? This week was just like last week? This year just like last year? Have you ever found yourself saying things like, well I will go on a holiday next year, or when our baby is born, or when I have more money? Do you get bored or find life monotonous at times? Do you feel like you are living Groundhog day? If you said yes to any of these, then you need a bucket list otherwise the next thing you know it will be too late. Without a bucket list you could find yourself lying on your deathbed with a ton of regrets – regretting all the things you didn't take the time to do that weren't urgent but important.

Life can be so much fun, an exciting adventure if we choose to step out of the ordinary and mundane and into the extraordinary. Many people live by default, reacting to the environment and their world, saying things like, "I can't afford that" or "when I win lotto". By completion of this book and upon becoming an athlete of the mind, you will begin to realise that when you choose what you want from life first, then take full responsibility for its attainment, it empowers you with a sense of controlling your own destiny. Some people say the sky's the limit, but is it really? Les Brown says, "Shoot for the moon. Even if you miss it you will land among the stars." If that doesn't inspire you, I'm not sure what will.

As you create your bucket list, your smorgasbord of delicious experiences you wish to have, it might be a challenge because we are not used to consciously having full freedom of choice or choosing anything our heart desires. A little voice inside your head might pop up and say things like, "you don't know how to do that" or "you don't deserve that" or other self-sabotage self-talk. This is not you, it's the brain's physiological response to not wanting to change, as it likes familiarity, it likes comfort, and it likes security.

When you are creating your bucket list and you hear that little voice (and you will), keep going because it means you are on track for the change that you truly desire. Remember that your brain is a part of you like your hand or your foot, and they can work unconsciously but you can also choose to consciously direct them.

For example, think of your big toe right now, now wiggle it, or don't. Now notice that before I brought it to your attention, you knew it was there right? Of course, but you weren't consciously thinking about it. Now you are, you can choose to move it any way you want, well your brain is the same, and it just takes time and practice, like crawling or even walking for the first time. The key here is daily consistency.

Creating a bucket list

I suggest starting by making a list of 26 magical memories you wish to create before you leave this world. Then what I suggest doing is then also making a list of 26 experiences you wish to create this year. The goal is to get you living your bucket list items once every two weeks, and then weekly. Imagine doing this even daily. These are the experiences that get you juiced, that get you excited, that just the sheer thought of get your heart beating faster and blood pumping.

You might be thinking, but Jason I like to be spontaneous and be free. At first I felt the same way, until I actually started living my bucket list and realised that by planning the memories I can live with more freedom, passion and adventure, quenching my thirst for my number one value in life; freedom!

You may also be thinking, well that's great Jason but I can't afford to travel and do all these eccentric or extravagant things. For now forget about the 'how to', and have faith in knowing that completing these steps with your why and what will give you the tools you need, that in time you will find a way. Know your why, manifest it and intensify it. Understand what you want (this process now), then determine and be flexible with your how.

Over the past 12 months I've had an incredible opportunity to travel to 12 countries and tick of over 140 bucket list items. Here are just a few of my favourite things that I've had the pleasure of experiencing that you may like to add to your own list:

Swim with dolphins

Swim with seals

Bathe an elephant

Go jet packing

Do aerobatics in a tiger moth plane

Meet Richard Branson

Visit Phi Phi Island

Visit Santorini Greek Islands

Sail the Greek Islands

Helicopter tour over Hawaii

Go hot air ballooning

Drink Sangria on Barcelona beach, Spain

Visit the Highlands in Scotland

Visit the Guinness brewery in Ireland

Visit the cliffs of Moher Ireland

Visit Positano Italy

Tuscany wine tour Italy

Visit Moet and Chandon Cellar in France

River cruise in Paris

Blue man show in Las Vegas

See the Hollywood sign

White water rafting in Indonesia

The Vatican in Rome

Jump from the Sky Tower in Auckland NZ

Visit Marina Bay Sands Singapore

Ride in a Gondola in Venice Italy

Travel the Golden Gate bridge San Fran

Disneyland with the family

Drive from Vegas to the Grand Canyon

Private island picnic with Kailey by Sea Plane

To assist you in creating your bucket list here are categories I suggest using:

- Material items you wish to have – Jet Ski, car, watch
- Things you wish to achieve – a degree, PhD, awards
- Places you wish to travel to – Egypt, Africa, Greece
- Things you wish to learn – a language, books, instrument
- People you would like to meet – celebrity, mentor, an inspiration
- Physical challenges you would like to experience – climb Mount Everest, iron man, triathlon
- Family memories you wish to create – take them somewhere or do something for them, marriage, children
- Experiences you wish to have – swim with dolphins, jet packing, hot air ballooning
- Charitable – start a charity, do events, get hands on in a third world country

Take the time now to write your bucket list items below.

My Top 26 Bucket List Items in Life

1) _____
2) _____
3) _____
4) _____
5) _____
6) _____
7) _____
8) _____
9) _____
10) _____
11) _____
12) _____
13) _____
14) _____
15) _____
16) _____
17) _____
18) _____
19) _____
20) _____
21) _____
22) _____
23) _____
24) _____
25) _____
26) _____

Once you have created these two lists, now it's time to prioritise them. I want to challenge you to stop whatever you are doing right now and book in your number one bucket list item on this list for two weeks from now. That's it – get on the phone, google it or do whatever you have to and BOOK IT RIGHT NOW!

Did you do it? Did you book it? How badly do you want to create your dream lifestyle and true happiness? You are right I cannot see you right now, but you are reading this book for a reason. You are not cheating me you are only cheating yourself of some potentially life changing experiences that create tremendous pleasure, make you feel your endorphins rushing and even those butterflies in the pit of your stomach that we remember forever. You are right, it's just one experience, it alone will not create long-term success or happiness. But it's a metaphor; a metaphor for what is possible for you in the future.

Now that you've booked your first bucket list experience (or have you?) the hardest part is done. Now you want to habituate ticking off an experience every two weeks. Imagine a life now, where you have 26-52 once in a lifetime experiences every year. What would that mean for you and your family? Imagine that over five years, ten years or even 40 years. WOW! The memories.

I cannot wait to hear your stories and would really love to see all the magnificent photos you take on your adventures whilst living your bucket list. Feel free to share them with us anytime online on our website or Fanpage.

SUGGESTION: Sit down with your partner or family and do this as a community exercise, nothing brings people closer than communicating about your hopes and dreams together, then actioning them.

> *There is no passion to be found playing small – in settling for a life that is less than the one you are capable of living.*
> —Nelson Mandela

Nada Kiblawi had a bucket list, her list included moving to the United States, the land of opportunity, and starting a business, but there was a major problem, she lived in a refugee camp.

An article by Karin Kamp (*The Story Exchange*, 2013) explains how Nada's family fled a Palestinian refugee camp for Lebanon in 1948 during the Arab-Israel war. They lost all of their land and possessions as a result.

The family ended up north of Beirut, in a United Nations refugee camp, where Nada and her whole family – six siblings and her parents – were allocated two rooms in the camp in less than desirable conditions.

They remained in the camp until Nada was in her early 20s and although it was a difficult experience, it helped shaped Nada's future.

Nada's father believed that education was the only way that his children could escape the refugee camp, so he worked hard crushing rocks to pave the streets, to ensure that his children could go to school.

Nada studied hard, in difficult conditions and managed to earn a scholarship to the American University of Beirut where she graduated at the top of her class and became the first woman to get an electrical engineering degree from the university.

Despite Nada's outstanding achievements at university she had trouble finding a job after graduation. As a Palestinian refugee, she was only allowed to work in certain jobs but when she attended graduate school and married a classmate, her life became more stable.

But her troubles weren't over when civil war broke out in Lebanon in 1975 and Nada and her husband escaped to Kuwait, where they managed to find engineering jobs and from there started a family.

In 1982, when Israel invaded Lebanon, again Nada feared for the safety of her family. Nada and her husband saw the United States as the land of opportunity and so they moved to America determined to provide a better life for their three children.

When I came across this story I thought WOW what a perfect example and proof that your environment does not ultimately determine what happens to you, but rather your choices. Nada refused to let her environment determine her destiny. When I was living on the streets many of the people I associated with are now dead or in prison because they let their environment determine their destiny. Just like myself and just like Nada you can change that and not be identified as a victim of your environment. Remember we are not trees, if we don't like where we are, we can move.

I understand if you are reading this from a country, prison or location you cannot escape that this may prove harder than just moving. We still need to take responsibility for our actions that lead us here, and from now we can change our actions through freedom of choice and direct our future that comes as a result of choice, our destiny. Nelson Mandela for nearly three decades was imprisoned yet he understood this better than anyone.

Creating a vision board

So you have created a bucket list, (you have right? Remember you're only cheating yourself) and it just sits there. You spend time, hours, even days creating this list and then it collects dust. You experience the fun of creating the list and dreaming about the experiences but you never action it and never really feel the pleasurable sensations of the real experience, and most importantly, the bonds and relationships it creates and strengthens with the people you care most about in this world.

My intention for this book is to give you the tools and resources you need to begin to create your dream lifestyle and motivate and inspire you to take massive action every day until you achieve them. One of the best mechanisms I know for this is accountability, even more powerful is public or social accountability. You've probably heard the saying, 'out of sight out of mind' right? So to keep you accountable to take action with your bucket list I suggest creating a vision board. You may have heard of a vision board, you might even already have one, but stick with me anyway as you might take something new on board.

Having a vision board and looking at it each morning when we first get up, and each evening before we go to bed, keeps our dream experiences in the forefront of our conscious mind. It is a visual display of all your dreams in one place that can give you laser beam focus, clarity and drive every day to get through the tough times.

To remember why you are doing what you are. Never quit on your dreams. Your vision board is a big part of your why, the fuel for the fire and when you take the time every morning and every evening to not just look, but also notice the feelings that arise when looking at the vision board and imagining yourself already having experienced those experiences associated through your own eyes. It makes what seems like a lifetime away to achieve more of a reality in the now. It feels good, exciting and even joyful. Now is an important time to remember that the brain doesn't recognise the difference between remembering the past, experiencing the present or imagining the future.

A vision board is essentially a Collage of all your big goals, dreams and bucket list experiences you wish to have. There are two ways I like to create a vision board:

1. The more traditional way is to invest in a large whiteboard and tripod for your bedroom. Then make a list of your top ten ultimate bucket list items, and your top ten bucket list items for this year, then find visual pictures in magazines, and papers you can cut out and stick on your board.

2. The strategy I use now as I constantly travel is to make a list of your top ten ultimate bucket list items, and your top ten bucket list items for this year, then find visual pictures on the internet you can add to a folder on your computer, laptop or tablet. Then you can play them as a slideshow each morning and evening.

Take the time now to determine and write down the top ten experiences you would like to have in your life and the top ten this year. If you were given ten days to live and you could have one experience a day and money was no object what would they be?

My Top 10 Vision Board Photos

1) _____   6) _____
2) _____   7) _____
3) _____   8) _____
4) _____   9) _____
5) _____   10) _____

My Top 10 Vision Board Photos For This Year

1) _____   6) _____
2) _____   7) _____
3) _____   8) _____
4) _____   9) _____
5) _____   10) _____

Both strategies are very effective, it's up to you as to which of the two options above are more practical for your current lifestyle. If you truly do want to create a dream lifestyle I believe this to be one of the most important starting action items to complete. Take the time to make your lists of ten right now, then once you are done I would love to see pictures or examples of your vision board that you can share with us online on our Fanpage or website.

Now your vision board and bucket list has been created we want to revisit it regularly and update it, as your confidence and ability grows in what you can achieve, your belief about your potential expands and you will automatically raise your standards and level of thinking.

I have found the most powerful way to keep you accountable to completing and using these two tools daily is to share it with your family, friends and loved ones. Yes, I agree we want to tell the world what we plan to do but first show it. However on my travels to refining this process as one of the most profound and impactful exercises in my life, I have discovered that by sharing my bucket list and vision board with the people that I want to be a part of it makes it more real. It also keeps you accountable to following through on your actions and delivering on your promises.

When I first moved to be with Kailey I made some huge promises and although she had faith and believed in me, I could still see in her eyes that the same certainty that I felt was missing in her. This encouraged me and motivated me in new and empowering ways you wouldn't believe. I knew my ferocity and tenacity for turning these dreams in the form of a bucket list and vision board into an incredible reality was emotionally fuelled by our ever growing true love.

This meant that I must make them real, I must do whatever it takes to follow through on my promises because I deeply love her and I'm a man of my word. Imagine if you did the same with your loved ones. Remember life is about creating a dream life with your loved ones, start the process yourself and don't be discouraged if even your loved ones don't have the same conviction and belief as you do, in time they will see you follow through and your words will have more credibility and conviction than ever, they will become truth.

Your words last just seconds, but your actions echo eternity!
—Jason Grossman

Visualising and seeing your future through your mind's eye as if you are living it now is the cornerstone of every success story of everyone that ever lived. Regardless of your beliefs about how it works or why it works there is no denying it does. Through prayer, meditation or visualisation we can begin to manifest and form our reality in the physical form from the seed we plant as thoughts. Religion talks about it, the bible talks about it, philosophers, sporting people, entertainers, businessmen and even quantum physicists talk about it. It appears it's one of the few things most super successful people can agree upon.

Regardless of your religious or non-religious views, visualising is quite possibly the most important part of beginning to turn your dreams into reality. Not just visualising but also emotionalising.

Here are a few names you might have heard of that have also used it to achieve incredible success and results in their lives.

Many successful and influential people use vision boards to encourage their success and to visualise their dreams. Oprah Winfrey is one of the most successful people to state that she uses vision boards and visualisation techniques as a practical tool for reaching goals.

It was in fact, the actor Jim Carrey that inspired Oprah to start using visualisation techniques.

On the *Oprah Show* in 1997, Jim Carrey told a story of how every night he used to drive to the top of a hill and visualise the things that he wanted in his life. At the time he was a struggling actor trying to make it in the business. In 1990 he wrote himself a cheque for $10 million and in the description field he wrote: *for acting services rendered*, which he dated for thanksgiving 1995. It remained in his wallet until just before Christmas 1995 when he found out that he was going to receive $10 million for his movie *Dumb and Dumber*, and the rest as they say, is history.

If you don't have a dream, there is no way to make one come true.

—Steven Tyler

Join the super successful and truly fulfilled today and begin to harness the awesome power of transforming your vision into reality through the accountability mechanisms of a bucket list and vision board. Remember you deserve a dream life, so does your family. Your dreams are possible, and the vision you create in your mind is the seed that you plant that can then grow into your fruitful future. Nourish, feed and water it through daily repetition until you form a magnificent obsession, sharing the exciting journey with the people you love most – then live and breathe it.

Creating a travel plan

Travel is the only thing you buy that makes you richer.
—Unknown

Would you like to travel more? Who doesn't? For many who desire creating freedom, more time and living their dream life, travelling is a huge part of that lifestyle. If I gave you $20,000 right now and you could go anywhere in the world, where would you go? Hawaii? Egypt? Greek Islands? Maldives? Paris? Somewhere else perhaps more exotic or secluded?

If you were to travel more, who would you take with you? Family? Partner? Kids?

Imagine if you were to have the opportunity to travel four times, yes that's right, four times a year.

Growing up we didn't have the opportunity to travel. In fact it was only 12 months prior to writing this book that I ever went overseas for the very first time. We have just been blessed with the incredible opportunity to have visited 12 countries in the last 12 months and we absolutely loved it. We would love to see pictures of your travels also so post them on our Fanpage or website. Some of the places we have visited in the last 12 months are Paris, Spain, the Greek Islands, Italy, Singapore, Bali, Thailand, California, Hawaii, Las Vegas, Ireland, Scotland, London and we are about to visit New York for New Year's then go to Fiji.

I share this not to impress you, but rather impress upon you, that I'm no different to you, if I can do it so can you. We are not super rich or multi-millionaires (yet). And you don't need to be to live a dream lifestyle. There are many super rich people that are unhappy – it's more than that. But I also understand you do need some money. If you can think it and you can dream it, then you can create a plan for it and transform that dream into a reality. It's not just possible, but highly probable with the right plan backed with massive action. This includes travelling the world and opening your mind to the possibilities of breathtaking views and once in a lifetime experiences. These experiences also allow you to create stronger bonds with your loved ones and relationships with such strong connections you've only ever dreamed of.

On our travels, the experiences we have had and the lessons we have learnt of history, culture and gratitude have been nothing short of incredible. These are things you cannot learn in your own country, a book or a classroom. Many people dream of travelling more, getting away and having holidays on the beach and in the sun, but many of us don't make it a priority yet. We say things like, well when I save money, or when I win lotto, or when I retire, when, when, when …

Whenever talking to people about creating a dream lifestyle, one of the things nearly everyone wishes to do more is travel. The challenge for some is getting away from their job, their business, other commitments, family, kids or financially it's not viable.

Well that's about to change for you. Because not only in this chapter are we going to help you create a travel plan and inspire you to travel at least four times a year, I'm also going to give you some resources to make it possible for you financially.

I would absolutely love to motivate you to make travel a much larger part of your life. We each have different reasons: refresh and recharge, create magical memories with loved ones, get away from the daily grind, make our family's and our own dreams come true. How many of your bucket list experiences do you wish to have that are in another country? Probably many.

Creating a travel plan and travelling more might sound nice, and you might like the idea of it, but it's probably not yet a large part of your life and a priority yet. You can still work, run a business and live a functional life and travel regularly.

Many other people simply just don't make it a priority. They don't have a plan to save or make money to cover the costs of travel and that's exactly what we will cover in this chapter, how to create the plan and action it. Then later in this book we will show you how to make residual income to feed your travel account to economically justify the places you wish to travel. How would that make travelling regularly more of a reality and possible for you?

Before we create this simple plan, I understand many people

will say things like, I would like to travel BUT ... I have other priorities, I can't afford it, I don't have the time etc.

I completely understand, but aren't you reading this book to gain a new perspective and outlook on life to create your dream lifestyle and success? If you don't wish to travel more then that's fine – don't, simply skip past this section. However, if you wish to travel more and create your dream lifestyle with magical memories with your loved ones then keep reading.

I'm going to show you how to make the time, how to prioritise it, how to plan it, and most importantly, how to pay for all the travel you wish to do.

With everyone I work with I begin by recommending just four trips a year. One trip overseas (at least four weeks long), one interstate (at least 3-5 days) and the other two are totally up to you. They could be a camping or fishing weekend away. As you find it easier to prioritise your travel, and get the proverbial bug, you can alter your plan to travel longer, more often or even four times a year overseas. Wow what a life.

Let's be honest, the only real thing stopping you from travelling more besides your own actions is money. If you had sufficient funds (residual income – without having to work), there wouldn't be much stopping you. Right? Sure, you may have kids in school, but imagine the learning they get have from touring ancient Rome and Italy for example, as opposed to reading about it in school. You might have a job, but if you had residual income you wouldn't even need that job, or you could work part-time so you could take the holidays. There is always a way if you are prepared to find one and ask the question: how do I make this happen? If you do have plenty of money, but you are poor on time, isn't it time to perhaps start prioritising time a little differently and creating some leverage in your life so you can spend quality time with your family and travel with them?

We are talking about your dreams here! You have already created your bucket list, so you will probably have a few destinations in mind. Take a breath and stop to take the time to follow these four simple steps now and begin your plan (Remember forget about the 'how to' for now and just go with the flow and create your plan as the how will come easily and naturally later):

1. Determine the four holidays you are going to go on this year, with departure and arrival dates.
2. Create a basic itinerary (simply start with just the international trip) by researching online for flights and accommodation, and also use this information to determine the cost of the entire trip for all people travelling (don't freak out).
3. Once you have the amount in total, we can then determine how much money you will need to make and save each week to cover the costs.
4. Set up a bank account (more details in the financial freedom section) specifically for your travels, and be sure to put the savings aside each week with a resource we will share with you.

Example: It is now August, and in six months time (January 5th) we will be travelling to the Maldives.

We will be staying there from 5th – 19th January (two weeks) – and I suggest looking for a specific hotel here.

Having looked online at flights, accommodation and expenses this will cost approximately $12,000 in total for two of us. $12,000 divided by six months ($12,000/26) = $461.53 a week we need to save. We now need to open a bank account called our travel account. THEN the fun begins. We need to create a financial plan on how we will make this money. That part will come in a later chapter, but for now simply create this part of the plan.

At first, like the bucket list you will follow this process, and that little voice will pop up again in your mind, you don't know how to do that, or you can't afford that, or you can't make that happen. Ignore that voice, I'm going to show you exactly just how you can make it happen.

If you have a partner, and/or family this is another great opportunity to do this exercise together. It's a great bonding exercise and by creating your itinerary together it makes it more of a reality. The brain doesn't recognise the difference between remembering the past, experiencing the now or visualising the future. It's all reality to the mind. So remember to be as detailed as possible when creating your plan and here are some steps to get you ahead.

Take the time now to answer these questions and begin to construct your exciting travel plans with your loved ones. Remember the power of public accountability as you do.

Where are the four places you wish to travel in the next 12 months? Once you determine each one be sure to sit down and follow the four steps on the previous page to imprint into the unconscious the realism and certainty of these trips.

Four Trips this year
1) Overseas:
2) Interstate:
3) Other:
4) Other:

We travel not to escape life, but for life not to escape us.
—Unknown

Once you have decided on your next four trips, let's turn your focus to the next overseas holiday or vacation. Take a moment now to answer the questions below then create a comprehensive plan with your family using the four steps on the previous page to make it a reality. Remember we will determine how you will fuel your economic status and bank account in the financial freedom chapter, for now simply create the plan on paper and in your mind with public accountability.

Overseas Trip

Destination(s) _____

Departure Day and Date _____

Return Day and Date _____

Cost of Flights _____

Cost of Accommodation _____

Place of Accommodation _____

Total Cost of Trip _____

Amount needed to save each week _____

    Now let's be sure to place the plan somewhere you will see it every day and remember to daily and weekly look at pictures, videos and information on that holiday to keep it in your mind's eye. We will complete the plan in the financial freedom chapter.

    What will it mean for you and your family if you were to experience the above four trips in the next 12 months? Why is that so important to you? How would you feel if in 12 months from now you are still where you are? BUT how would you feel if you took action today, created the plan and began to travel the world with the people you love the most? Feel free to create this plan with all four of your trips as we strongly recommend. Once you read the financial freedom chapter, be sure to action everything and book your dream trips today!

Travel is like love, mostly because it's a heightened state of awareness, in which we are mindful, receptive, undimmed by familiararity and ready to be transformed. That is why the best trips, like the best love affairs, never really end.

—Pico Iyer

    How would you like to save thousands of dollars on travel? Kailey and I saved almost $20,000 last year alone because of a VIP Travel Club we are a part of. If you plan to travel, trust me when I say by being a part of this VIP Travel Club you will get the cheapest flights and accomodation in the world. To discover more about the travel club simply visit www.streetstoamillionaire.com

Many psychologists and therapists have even said and offered scientific research on how changing your environment, especially at extreme levels in culturally diverse countries is one of the most effective strategies for eliminating depression. Many in the NLP and hypnosis world also agree, as do I.

Completing your dream lifestyle design plan

On completion of your bucket list, vision board and travel plan, I'm sure you will have other goals and aspirations, however as you become more masterful through using these three strategies daily you will find you can begin to use the three elements for pretty much any part of your life. Writing a business plan can be boring and mundane, so not only does this strategy promote the way the brain works anyway with images, feelings and sensory data but it also makes the planning process much more exciting, not to mention it gives you a project to work on with loved ones.

If you visit our website www.streetstoamillionaire.com you can find additional tools, resources and worksheets if you are the sort of person that would like to be even more logistic and specific in your planning.

Without goals, and plans to reach them, you are like a ship that has set sail with no destination.

—Fitzhugh Dodson

4

WINNING THE INNER-OUTER GAME OF LIFE

I believe winning the game of life is about mastering communication, communicating effectively with oneself, with others and the world around us to create a harmonious alliance connecting each as one.

—Jason Grossman

We live in a world of duality. Hot and cold, up and down, in and out, happy and sad, yin and yang. We've heard sayings like 'opposites attract' and most of us have a basic understanding of how magnetisation works or at least that it does. So what does all this mean and how can we use it in the achievement of true fulfilment and living our dreams?

At this stage you are clear on your why (if you completed the exercises) and you have created your dream lifestyle design plan. It seems it is now logical to start taking action, right? As Abraham Lincoln once said, "Give me six hours to chop down a tree and I will spend the first four hours sharpening the axe." Instead of now picking up the axe and madly cutting at the tree of life and your dreams, it's important to sharpen your mind and understand that we are constantly living simultaneously in two worlds.

If you stop and think about it for a moment you will realise this is true. We do in fact live in two worlds simultaneously. We are constantly living in the world of our thoughts and internal representations, emotions, beliefs, values, feelings and at the same time we are also living in the outer world of the weather, economy, other people, environment, traffic etc.

This is a very common presupposition or belief in the NLP world and has become more popular over recent years as too has NLP itself. It's very clear that we are obviously living in two worlds simultaneously, but what does it all mean, and how can you use this to enhance your results in life? How can you use this principle to win the outer game of success and the inner game of fulfilment?

If you will allow me to I'm going to use a metaphor, the metaphor: life is a game. Many of us use metaphors a lot more than we realise and many of these metaphors will actually shape our perception of reality and beliefs. Some people might say that life is a party, or life is a dance or even life is a war. Think about the presuppositions and other beliefs that would automatically be attached to and accompany those metaphors.

For this chapter we are going to use the metaphor that life is a game. Like all metaphors it has its positives and its negatives, because if you truly do believe that life is a game then games have losers, therefore it's possible that one can lose the game of life. However we can then choose to adjust the synergistic beliefs that accompany it like making the definition of losing the game of life so hard it seems impossible to lose. Let me explain. If we were to sit in a room of 20 people right now and ask them each to write down on a piece of paper their definition of success, would they not all be different definitions? If we then opened up the dictionary and read the definition of success in the dictionary there is a very good chance that definition would be completely different again. Does that mean that you and the other 19 people are wrong? Does that make the dictionary right? Of course not, because the word success is known as a nominalisation in linguistics, which simply means that it's not tangible. It's not a real thing as you cannot put success into a wheelbarrow, right? So the mind attempts to understand this non-specificity and gives it its own meaning semantically.

Take a few minutes now to write down your definition of success below. Be sure to say it in a way that you could prove it to someone else and make it measurable. Also make it so easy that it's almost impossible that you cannot succeed. Example: my definition of success is to improve every day in the five main areas of my life: Finances, Health, Relationships, Mindset and Spirituality.

My definition of success is:

_____

_____

_____

_____

_____

So to give this chapter some context and meaning we will refer to the metaphor life is a game, ensuring we are in the same page. We are also going to use my personal belief that the only way to lose (or fail) in life is to quit. I know I will never, ever, ever quit on my dreams and my legacy therefore the only way I can really lose the game of life is to die. Well none of us are getting out of life alive anyway so we may as well play the game at 100%.

So if the only way I can lose the game of life is to quit or die (which we all do one day anyway, so is it really losing?) I cannot truly lose. However that then raises the question of, what is winning the game of life and how do I win? That too is up to you, it depends on your standards and your values, and your definition of winning the game of life, how important things are to you and what level you are prepared to play at.

Take the time now to write down your definition of failure and make it so hard it seems impossible to fail.

My definition of failure is:

_____

_____

_____

If life consists of two worlds, the inner game and the outer game, at what level are you playing? Are you playing at beginner? Intermediate? Perhaps advanced? Maybe there's even a level above advanced, and even above that!

If you were to make a list right now of the top five people you believe are winning the game of life, what specifically causes you to believe they are winning? Money? Fame? Family? Values? Just as it is critical for you to know your definition of success and a dream life, you must also know your definition of winning the game of life. Winning the inner game and winning the outer game with synchronicity and balance. In the remainder of this book I'm going to share with you the lessons I've learnt along the way from NLP, hypnosis, quantum physics, psychology, my own mistakes, failures and successes to empower you with motivation and the ability to raise your standards, play a bigger game and move through the ranks of how advanced you are playing the inner-outer game of life. I guess you could say this book is a manual on how to win the game of life! Are you up for the challenge to think larger, act more, do more, be more? Not just for you but for your family; your community. Life is a blessing and a privilege; life-force itself is a power and with power comes responsibility. Pardon the Spiderman pun.

Notice the hyphen (-) between inner-outer game, why is it there? Have you wondered? Maybe you haven't, maybe you have. Well the reason it's there is because like the mind-body connection where the mind cannot survive without the body and the body cannot survive without the mind (well without technology anyway), they affect each other and are linked. We cannot experience the inner world without the outer world, and we definitely cannot experience the outer world without the inner world, and they too have an effect on one another.

I believe winning the game of life is mastering your communication and interaction within the inner world between your conscious and unconscious focusing on your four internal powers (which we will cover later in the book). At the same time also mastering your communication and interaction with the outer world that scientists often refer to as the quantum field, which spiritual people might call the universe and religious people may call god.

These are the powerful tools I and thousands of successful and fulfilled people before you have used to win the inner-game of life. Have you ever heard about a celebrity that seems to have all the money in the world, success and fame yet is miserable? In fact how many have overdosed or even committed suicide? They may be appearing to win the outer game but I'm sure you would agree that they are definitely not winning the inner game of life.

Have you ever known someone or met someone that seems to be always happy and grateful and fulfilled yet they struggle to pay their bills, form long lasting relationships or seem stuck in their environment? They may be winning the inner game but are they really winning the outer game? Some people believe it's bad to be religious or spiritual and win the outer game, to be rich, travel a lot and create financial freedom and wealth. Was this your belief up until now?

You don't have to be really rich to win the outer game, nor do you need to be a monk to win the inner game. However they both do take work and by the end of this book you will have a much deeper understanding of how to easily and effortlessly win the inner-outer game of life to create inner peace and true fulfilment and at the same time create financial freedom and travel the world.

The two people that first come to mind for me that I believe won the inner-outer game of life are Richard Branson and Nelson Mandela. Probably the two most inspiring and impactful people that without them even knowing have been great mentors for me.

Nelson Mandela and Richard Branson. Although in many ways they would be considered very different they were at no surprise to me good friends with one another, in fact I remember reading somewhere Nelson Mandela would never miss the opportunity to call Sir Richard Branson every birthday. I remember when Nelson Mandela passed away I actually broke down in tears, my partner Kailey did not know what to do as she had never seen me like this before. His strength, his leadership, his understanding of the inner-outer game and the legacy he left. I fell to a heap on the couch and blubbered like a child thinking to myself what I have ever done to make a difference, when he has done so much and given so much to this world. If I could do even 1% of what he has done for the people and this earth it would be more than a privilege.

Although he probably won't remember, I had the opportunity to meet Richard Branson at a fundraiser a few years back in Perth, Western Australia. It was a VIP event for around just 200 people at the Indiana tea house looking over Cottesloe beach. I heard someone say, "he's coming" and we all looked out on the beach and there was Richard Branson coming towards the shore in style on his kite surf. He came to shore, ripped off his wetsuit to reveal his white linen shirt and shorts, jumped up on stage with his hair still dripping wet and continued by saying, "okay let's do this!"

I had the opportunity to have a quick chat with him, and the aura of confidence that he oozes was incredible. He then held a magical after party I will forever remember as one of the best nights of my life.

You can see below the photo from that fundraiser with his hair still wet. I look like a deer in headlights! What an inspiring man with a great heart and electrifying aura.

Victory at all costs, victory in spite of all terror, victory however long and hard the road may be; for without victory there is no survival.

—Winston Churchill

Who inspires you? Make a list of the top five people you believe are winning the game of life. Then follow their blog, fan page and website and visit it every day. Read their autobiography and all their books. In NLP they call this modelling. They say that if we take the top five people we spend the most time with, then average their income, that will be ours. We will also adopt their beliefs, values and habits. Start modelling people that inspire you and you are driven to be like. That will bring out the best in you.

I've been following Richard Branson for some time now and not a day goes by where I don't check out what he is doing. His passion for helping others and this planet is amazing. At the moment I have noticed he is focusing a lot on marine life. What are you passionate about? How can you make a difference? His passion for the future of mankind and this planet is second to none, one I believe we can all draw inspiration from.

As we have role models, so too do we have reverse role models and they can be just as important for learning from their mistakes and for what not to do. To win the outer game of life we really need to rid ourselves of any experiences or influences holding us back from achieving our dreams. Watching the news, listening to the radio and reading the newspaper are a great place to start eliminating these habits. "It was the best of times, it was the worst of times" (Charles Dickens). We've all heard this. What does this mean? Well it's really simple. Right now someone is being murdered, raped, stabbed, killed, terrorised or molested. My apologies for that visual. However, right now someone is saving a life, doing something heroic, helping with an act of kindness, putting a smile on someone's face or creating something beautiful that we will remember for centuries.

What we focus on expands and what we focus on we feel. The key to beginning to win the game of life is to begin to control and direct your own conscious mind (the inner game) and choose what you experience in your outer game. We experience the outer game through our five senses. Visual, kinaesthetic, auditory, olfactory and gustatory; sight, feeling, sound, smell and taste. This is the only way we can experience. We experience through these five mechanisms so we can live harmoniously with the outer world (so-called reality) and interact with it. We see something outside of us in the outer world, then due to refraction of light streaming through the eye and the visual cortex it is imprinted and we see. Then we give it meaning.

As we experience millions of distinctions (some people even say billions) every second, the conscious mind needs to filter what's important so it deletes, distorts and generalises, chunking it down to bite size pieces of information that the conscious mind can handle. Everything else creeps straight into the unconscious. What's creeping into your unconscious? We then give this image (or other sensory experience) meaning through associating it with something else (normally an internal response of some kind). This is why for many people removing judgement from their habitual character can be so difficult. To look into the eyes and soul of a person and see them for their beauty, light and energy that they are, rather than projecting onto them. Or looking at a beautiful flower and just appreciating it as it is.

By now you are probably thinking this is great Jason but what does all this mean or have to do with my success? Well it's really simple. At the end of the day we are all fully responsible for what happens in our inner world and our outer world, the problem is that many people just live by default, they have been conditioned to react rather than respond to both their inner world and outer world. They become a product of their environment and can play the victim, and are helpless with no ability to make changes in their life rather than making their environment become a product of them and shaping their own destiny.

Emotions are not good or bad they are simply signals, telling us whether we are getting what we want from life or not. And when we experience a stimulus in the outer world like someone driving down the street and cutting you off. Many people might react by flipping the bird, and getting angry. But why give them 30 seconds or more of your happiness? Why empower them with the ability to determine how you feel? Imagine a life where everyone walked around allowing what people said or the way they were treated determine how they felt. You will never feel in control of how you feel. You could never win the game of life.

Besides for every 60 seconds you are sad or angry you lose one minute of happiness. I don't know about you but I would rather choose to be happy and shape my environment than let others determine how I feel and my environment shape me. Wouldn't you agree?

Winning the outer inner-outer game means you understand you have an opportunity between stimulus and response to respond (response-ability) through conscious choice rather than reacting through unconscious conditioning. Which will you choose from now?

When elephants are born in captivity in Thailand to be trained, the trainers (although cruel and I don't agree with it) wrap a chain around the baby elephant's leg and peg it into the ground. The baby elephant will cry for sometimes hours on end trying to break free from the chain until it eventually just gives up and forms a belief that it cannot break free and it is futile to even try. As the elephant becomes fully mature and grows, it no longer even attempts to break free from this chain and the trainer just wraps a loose rope around the leg of the elephant with a small peg in the ground. The elephant does not realise that it could easily break free from that rope, and flee to freedom but doesn't even try because it is a prisoner of its own conditioning and belief that was formed at a younger age.

What old chains could you easily break free from today? What chains are holding you back? Everything you have in your life right now is a direct reflection of the beliefs you have. What beliefs are acting like chains holding you back and stopping you from creating freedom in your life? Stopping you from creating a dream life where you can win the inner-outer game of life?

Now, imagine you walk into a dark room, and let's pretend that dark room is your unconscious mind. Then you pull out a torch and shine the torch. Wherever the torch shines and you focus on is your conscious mind, everything else is your unconscious. Many people do not control or at least direct their torch and definitely have no idea where to shine it, so they carelessly wave it backwards and forwards. However those that are focused on winning the inner-outer game focus strongly with intention on those areas where they shine their torch.

As Gregory Bateson said, "Energy flows where attention goes as determined by intention!"

Isn't it time you took control of your torch? Isn't it time you choose to take responsibility for your life, take control and choose a life you dream of and make it a reality? By the way will you use a cheap nasty torch, or a powerful and bright torch with a long life battery?

To truly win the inner-outer game of life, I believe that we want to have balance between the two worlds for true success and happiness. Besides that is generally how the universe works. Everything in the end balances out, that's how life is possible. It's like a seesaw. If you are winning the outer game you could be lonely and miserable on the inside, just like if you are winning the inner game you could be broke and struggling financially.

Now I'm not saying you need to be rich to be happy, I'm simply suggesting that in today's world if you want to live a dream lifestyle where you can create magical memories with the people you love, then financial abundance is not just important, but necessary. Imagine how you could also help others on a larger scale if you had financial abundance. Relationships and leverage are also critical to win the outer game. Don't you want to master both worlds so you can feel completely fulfilled and live a dream lifestyle? Sometimes all it takes is for someone to come along and say yes you are content, perhaps even happy, but if you are being really honest are you truly fulfilled?

You deserve to be rich and wealthy, just as you deserve to feel fulfilled. You can have your cake and eat it too, many people do it, it is possible.

We've all heard of the three components that make up our physical being. Body, mind and soul. Some people also refer to them as mind, body and spirit. Regardless of belief systems most people agree that we have each of these three in some way, shape or form.

The body and mind are easy as we can touch our body and we can think, therefore to us they exist. They are real. The soul and/or the spirit isn't as simple or as seemingly real to many, however some say it is a gateway. A gateway to heaven, a communication gateway to a higher power or even a gateway to the universe. Heck even atheists believe in something like a soul and/or spirit. You know that unexplainable part of you that gets that gut feeling like something just feels right? Or not right? Have you ever had that feeling before? Some call that the soul. Maybe that's what the soul is, that part of us that connects our mind and body to everything else that we cannot experience through one of our five senses, hence why sometimes it's called our sixth sense. It connects us to that thing we cannot explain through using our five senses.

Firstly there is the body as energy and how to maximise your body's energy for longevity and results. Secondly mindset. We will talk about the four powers of the mind and mental vitamins you can take to align your psychology for success and become an athlete of the mind. Thirdly we will also talk about the soul, regardless of your own personal beliefs being that unexplainable part we cannot experience through our five senses as character traits and the part of the inner game that leads to inner peace by using the four keys to true fulfilment. This stuff might seem a little deep to you at first, but I promise if you take the time to read it you will be very glad you did. Besides I swear it's not too airy fairy. How badly do you want to create your dream lifestyle? What are you prepared to do? Are you hungry? Let's do this together. I'm not saying it's going to be easy, but it will be simple, and it will be worth it.

Later in this book we will also cover what I believe to be the most important elements required for mastering and winning the outer game. Firstly creating financial freedom, secondly creating leverage and harnessing the power of the four types of leverage and thirdly the seven most impactful universal laws we need to understand to win the outer game.

On completion of this book and its exercises you will have all the tools, resources and knowledge you need to win the inner-outer game of life and achieve your definition of success and fulfilment.

Some might even say success is what we achieve in the outer game and fulfilment is what we achieve in the inner game. It's time to start living the life of your dreams.

Billions of people are going to die not even having taken a single step
towards achieving their dreams let alone actually living them.
Who will you be?

—Jason Grossman

A massive thank you to Richard Branson for being such a massive inspiration and role model and being one of the very few people in this world that I believe have won the advanced level inner-outer game of life.

According to biography.com, Richard Branson was born 18 July 1950, in England. He struggled with dyslexia and as a result he had a hard time at school and dropped out at the age of 16 and started a youth magazine called *Student*.

The magazine was run by students and managed to sell $8000 worth of advertising in the first edition. The first print run of 50,000 copies was distributed for free with the costs being covered by the money made from advertising.

Whilst living in London Branson had the idea of a mail-order record company called Virgin to help financially fuel his magazine. Although starting the business modestly he was able to expand the business adding a record shop in London and also building a recording studio in 1972.

After growing Virgin Music to one of the top six record companies in the world, Branson expanded his company even further by branching out into the travel industry with the launch of the Voyager group, Virgin Atlantic and a bunch of Virgin Mega-stores.

The Virgin Group now includes over 200 companies in over 30 countries, including the United Kingdom, the United States, Australia and Canada. The Virgin Group continues to thrive now including a train company, a mobile phone company and a space-tourism company, Virgin Galactic, just to name a few.

What an incredibly inspiring man, a man I call a mentor and a true entrepreneur. If you haven't taken the time yet to read his book *Losing my Virginity*, it's definitely well worth the read.

Winning means you're willing to go longer, work harder, and give more than anyone else.

—Vince Lombardi

5

4 KEYS TO TRUE FULFILMENT

We cannot control everything we get, only what we give, therefore our power truly lies in giving; the giving of our love, life and gifts to create happiness in the hearts of the lives we touch!

—Jason Grossman

In my last (if being brutally honest) unsuccessful business – well it was successful financially but that's the only way – we ended up with a team of 16 including personal trainers, coaches, nutrition-ists and other experts. I had spent two years self-absorbed by the business and my only focus in life was making money. One day I took all the team on an outing I used to call 'team adventure'. We hired bicycles and rode up the west coast of Australia (or maybe it was down) and stopped at the most famous pubs for a drink. At one of the pubs everyone was so happy. They were all talking about how it was the best job they've ever had, how great life was and how awesome they felt about everything.

This was the very moment I realised that I was utterly miserable. I created a business that worked financially but I was the most depressed I had been in many years. I started to self-sabotage the business and started by randomly firing a few of the team members for no reason at all. I started making a lot of irrational and emotional decisions and was clearly taking it out on the team and the business. When I closed that business down to move to be with Kailey the way I went about everything was not in alignment with my values and as a result it created guilt and pain.

We all make mistakes, forgive yourself, forgive others, don't make the same mistakes again, learn from them and become a better human being every single day. When I met Kailey, she opened my eyes and reminded me what was really important in life, which is what I want to share with you openly in this book.

The title of this chapter may sound a little deep to you but don't you want to feel good? Doesn't everyone? Don't you want to feel happier or even more fulfilled? Who doesn't want more happiness and fulfilment in their life? What is fulfilment though and how do we experience it at any time?

Many people seek success in the hopes to become happy but I truly believe that success without fulfilment is failure. What's the point of having money, success and even travelling and creating bucket list if you are not happy or fulfilled? Having someone to share it with and relationships are crucial.

Many people go through life depressed, sad and unhappy. Some people go through life being content and some even happy. But very few live a life of true fulfilment. You don't have to be incredibly spiritual or religious to feel fulfilment. Fulfilment is a choice we make and is available to all of us.

I have certainly been guilty in the past of attempting to overcome my boredom or create happiness through instant gratification. Drugs, sex, gambling, shopping, eating, alcohol, even exercise are often used to mask our sadness, depression and/or boredom. The problem is that these are measured along a different continuum and although may distract us for a moment, they do not create long-term true fulfilment. What memories and feelings stay with you longer? A one night meaningless intimate experience or an experience of saving someone's life? I remember when I was young, a friend overdosed on heroin and we had to commence EAR and CPR. Later we discovered that if we hadn't she would have died. Another experience I had was one day when I heard a dog yelping in intense pain from a few houses across from us, after almost 60 minutes I jumped the fence to find out what was happening. It turned out the dog had slipped through a crack in the fence and a piece of wire had penetrated all the way through its leg and out the other side. I helped it free, contacted the RSPCA and remember the feelings still to this day of saving that dog's life.

I'm not saying don't have fun, I'm the first to say let's go do something thrilling, all you need to do is look at my bucket list. It's simply important to understand the difference between pleasure, happiness and fulfilment and why you seek it.

What is happiness and fulfilment to you? How do you know when you feel happy or fulfilled? And what's the difference between happiness and fulfilment? Emotions are not something we experience out there in the outer world, they are something we experience internally, in here. You cannot feel happiness outside of your body, can you? I'm sure you will agree the only place you can feel happiness or anything for that matter is within you. Emotions can be measured along a continuum, they are analogous, they are not something we do or do not feel, or digital (something we can switch on and off) like a light switch. We are always emoting and feeling, you cannot, not feel unless you are dead. Ever wished you could just stop feeling? That's called death.

We feel feelings at different levels like on an old TV you can turn the dial clockwise to turn the volume up or anti-clockwise to turn the volume down. It's measured along a scale of volume. For example one-ten. Just like you can turn the volume up on the TV, you can increase the intensity of your emotions or what you feel. As you read this imagine a straight line along a page and on the very left is severe depression, as we increase the level moving to the right of that line the depression becomes milder, then slightly unhappy and sad and then we continue to the centre of the line for a neutral state where we are not happy or sad. Some may call this contentment, maybe something else. Then we can begin to move the dial to the right of the line and feel slight happiness and build it all the way to incredible fulfilment. What if I told you there is a way you can begin to choose to control and direct this dial? Would that interest you to keep reading? Wouldn't you rather choose the volume on your TV? Then surely you would want to choose your emotions too?

Some people say happiness is when we subordinate our feelings to our values (what's most important to us). For example, imagine you are sick with the flu and you are in bed. It's your mum or dad's birthday and you don't want to miss it. You are really sick but do you still attend? Most people would say yes and that is because family is probably your number one or one of your top values. You know that if you don't go you will feel guilty and that will create more pain than being sick, and besides you will still be sick if you go (or will you?). However if you go you know you will still be sick, but you will be living congruently with your values and your parents will be happy and so shall you. Living congruently with our values and acting in alignment with them creates inner peace. It creates fulfilment. When we don't it creates negative states, emotions and feelings.

But what if there is something more than being content or even happy. Some people would tell you that there is. Sometimes all it takes is for the right person to come along and say, yes you are right, you are content and you are happy but are you really, truly fulfilled? Be honest with yourself are you truly, madly and deeply fulfilled in every aspect and element of your life and soul? Isn't there at least one area of your life you wish to improve?

Fulfilment really is just a word, it's a manmade label we have given to attempt to describe something that doesn't really exist. It's a feeling, it's intangible, and we cannot put it into a wheelbarrow, so it only exists within us not out there. In NLP it is known as a nominalisation, another manmade label. In fact if we are really honest here I'm not even Jason. Jason is simply a label my parents gave me so when I was in trouble I would know they were talking to me (haha!). Also legally for referencing and other legalities a name is required. But what if my parents called me Bob or Andrew? I am so much more than that label, and you are so much more than the name/label your parents gave you. We are human beings, a beaming light of energy, and that's just the beginning. It's very easy to be seduced by identifying ourselves with those labels when we are so much more. Fulfilment as a word, label and nominalisation will have a different meaning for each of us, and we will all feel it at different times and in different ways. Fulfilment as a whole is so much more than that label or word. Just as we are. Fulfilment is a way of being.

What if someone played a trick on you, and as a child told you that blue was red and red was blue? Then when you arrived in high school or even into adulthood no matter what anyone else said or told you there was nothing they could do or say to convince you that you are wrong and have the colours back to front. The truth is that neither of you are right or wrong, as it's simply an agreement that a majority of the population have agreed it to be correct and turned it into a fact. Neither colour is red or blue, in fact, to many creatures they wouldn't even appear as blue or red, we simply perceive it this way because of the way light filters through the rods and cones within our eyes. Psychologists say we are wrong 95% of the time. But how would you even know if you were wrong? If you knew you were wrong, you would be right, right? What other manmade labels are holding you prisoner and stopping you from achieving your dreams and feeling fulfilled?

Freedom comes from the liberation experienced when we understand that nothing has any meaning but the meaning we give it. If that's the case no one is ever right or ever wrong (in their own minds); this is a hard concept to grasp. You say, well what about facts Jason? They exist!

Well once upon a time it was a fact that the world was flat, once upon a time it was a fact that the sun revolved around the earth. Imagine what else we know now, which may not really be true. I'm not suggesting going around not believing things, I'm simply suggesting how important it is to understand that you have a freedom of choice, to believe or not believe and challenge the status quo. Besides isn't that how all great inventions and breakthroughs in society are made?

You may believe this, you may not. Again that's your choice. You shouldn't believe everything I say anyway, it's up to you to openly absorb information and make up your own mind. Beliefs aren't right or wrong they simply serve us or not. What beliefs are holding you back and what beliefs do you not yet have that are necessary for you to turn your dreams into reality and feel incredibly fulfilled? They are different for everyone, and it all starts with the freedom of choice.

After studying literally hundreds of successful people that have faced adversity to not only overcome it but create true success in the outer world but more importantly true fulfilment and turn my life around so drastically, personally, I have noticed that there are four keys to true fulfilment. These are not my creation and I certainly cannot take credit for them, I've simply exposed them by modelling people I believe are truly fulfilled at the core. These people understand fulfilment is not a destination, it's a journey, and it's something you can choose to feel at any time. Yes you want to learn from the past and plan for the future but truly fulfilled people understand it's really about living in the now. Eckhart Tolle understands this and writes much more eloquently than I ever will be able to in his book *The Power of Now*. If you haven't read that book yet, I highly recommend that you do. The key here is daily consistency.

I'm about to share with you these four keys that you can begin to use easily and naturally today to feel true fulfilment. If you choose to use and apply these four keys every single day, I guarantee that this chapter in this book alone will change your life in ways you could only ever dream of before today. As you read with great interest and find yourself easily becoming captivated by what the four keys are and how simple they are, you will also begin to understand that these four keys will not guarantee that you will feel fulfilled. What will guarantee that you feel fulfilled is the daily never ending application and use of all four keys.

I'm going to give you these four keys on a key ring now and if you choose to use each key, you can unlock and effortlessly walk through each of the four doors to true fulfilment and feel fulfilled at any time of the day. It will take time to condition your mind at first to remember to use these four keys everyday for the rest of your life. It's like learning to drive a car, at first you have to remember to signal and look but now you don't even think about driving you just do it, right? You build unconscious competence and that is what will happen for those that choose to use these four keys everyday, before too long you are automatically applying these unconsciously everyday from here forth.

Success is meaningless without fulfilment – both begin within.
—Rasheed Ogunlaru

The first key to true fulfilment

Just before Christmas in November 2013 I booked one of my biggest bucket list items and I was so excited I could barely sleep. I booked an aerobatic experience on a 1979 tiger moth, (you know the cool old school aerobatic planes with open cockpits). I remember having just a few hours sleep when my partner, a friend of hers and I got up early for the 45 minute drive on the Gold Coast, Australia. We then arrived on what appeared like a farm with a huge field, and in the distance I could see the shinning red and silver plane and my heart jumped a beat. The pilot went through the safety procedures and then I hopped in the front as he put my helmet and goggles on. He asked if I was ready and I replied with a swift hell yes. The flight lasted around 45 minutes and the barrel roles, and backward flips we did made me chuckle and laugh out loud like a little kid. To this day it is still one of the most incredible things I have ever done. I was so excited and proud I posted the photos online and thanked the company on their Facebook fan page.

The next day I received a phone call. It was from a news reporter. The news reporter asked me how I felt about what happened. I didn't understand what she was talking about at first. She then went on to tell me that the very next day, the next two people in that very same plane, crashed and were both killed instantly. I was shocked, a flood of mixed emotions surged like electricity through my body. They asked to do a news story in which I simply offered my condolences to all the family and friends of the two in the plane and all involved.

When I first received the news, I went out to the balcony of our then Surfers Paradise hotel room and stood overlooking the picturesque view. I took a big deep breath and found myself contemplating. Did I feel lucky that it could have been me and it wasn't? Not at all. I felt the most intense feeling of gratitude I had ever felt in my entire life. For two-three minutes, what felt like a lifetime, I found myself not thinking, but just feeling grateful and being in the moment and at one with my surroundings! Noticing what I could see, smell and hear and being grateful for life and all the experiences my five senses allowed me to experience. I then found myself feeling very grateful for the people in my life, my sweetheart, family, friends and business community. My heart and soul still go out to everyone involved, and the next day when I saw the plane that I was on just a few days before in pieces on TV it really sunk in. You can see photos of the plane and I below.

A happy snap of myself with the beautiful Tiger Moth on the Gold Coast in Australia.

Getting ready to take off in the Tiger Moth, little did I know I would
be the last person alive inside it.

If you haven't worked it out yet, the very first key to true fulfilment is gratitude. Truly fulfilled people are grateful for everything
that they already have in their lives. No matter how small or large.
They understand accumulating or getting more stuff will not make
them happy especially if they are not even grateful for what they
do have.

Being grateful also forces us to live more in the now and be
present, the only time and place you can feel anything is in the
now. The only power you have to influence anything is in the now.
You cannot change the past and the future has not yet happened
within our realm of experience.

How would you like to stop worrying, eliminate stress and
remove doubt and anxiety from your life? If you keep reading I'm
going to show you exactly how you can do just that at any time you

like within a matter of 60 seconds.

Why do we feel worry or stress? It's really simple, it's because we are thinking about what might go wrong in the future, or about what might happen in the future. You are worried about how well things are going to go, whether you are going to be good enough, or will things go to plan.

To stop feeling stress, worry, anxiety or uncertainty, the key is gratitude. By asking ourselves just two simple questions we can draw our attention from the future and bring us to the now. This empowers us with the ability to focus on what we can control rather than what we cannot. It causes us to be solution-focused (living in the present) rather than problem-focused (the past or future). Are there times when we want to revisit the past? Of course, it's important for learning. Are there times when we want to visit the future in our minds? Definitely, when visualising and planning our dreams, goals and future. But the only power you have to act and feel is in the right now. Besides, when is now a good time to do anything?

As Wayne Dyer says: "The past has already taken place so we cannot change that so we don't need to worry about it anymore. The future hasn't happened yet so no need to waste time on worrying about that. That just leaves the now, and there's nothing to worry about in the now. So therefore there's nothing at all to worry about." As you sit there reading this, ask yourself the question: is there anything to worry about right this very moment in your current experience where you sit? Do you not have food? Shelter? Warmth? Safety? A good book? By switching our focus to uptime and noticing what we can see, hear and feel, it takes us out of our own mind and judgement and places us in just being, in the now.

Next time you feel worry, stress or anxiety, take a deep breath and ask yourself these two questions:

1) What and who am I most grateful for in my life right now?

This breaks our state and interrupts the recursive loop pattern that seems to just intensify the more we think about it and draws our focus to the now.

2) Who do I love and who loves me?

Gratitude and love go hand in hand. In fact when you use the potent combination of real love and gratitude it will even eliminate fear.

Once we have interrupted the pattern and drawn your attention to the now, to be solution-focused, and once we have negated the negative thought process we can then switch the negative to a positive which will be covered in the second key.

So, next time you feel worry or stress, simply notice and accept it and you will probably realise that it is something in the future that hasn't even happened yet. Ask yourself the questions: what and who am I most grateful for right now? Who do I love and who loves me? And begin to notice the worry and stress be replaced with a warm fuzzy feeling that causes you to live in the present and be more resourceful.

Truly fulfilled people that are grateful for what they have in their life are grateful for it no matter how infinitesimal it seems. If they have ten dollars to their name they focus on being grateful for the fact that they have ten dollars as there are people out there in massive debt, feeling so overwhelmed that they are even contemplating suicide.

When we visited Bali in Indonesia. We visited a place called Ubud and there were people with their entire families living in small manmade huts that they had built themselves from the plantation around them. They had no money and barely any food. They would literally work the entire day just to pay for food for them and their family. Yet when we walked or drove through there they were always smiling and very grateful people. I believe it's because they focus on what's really important, their family values are priority. They don't focus on what they don't have, they focus on what they do have. They are still some of the happiest people I've ever met not burdened by a lot of first world country pressures or seductions. The lessons I personally learnt about gratitude in Bali I could never have learnt in my own country of Australia or in a book, and I'm so grateful for the experiences and culture we experienced with them personally. I think that some of us can be a bit spoilt, we don't realise how easy we have it in Australia, or other developed countries. Strength grows from resistance and I believe it is no co-incidence that the super successful people in this world are those who have faced up against adversity to beat all the odds. They have experienced some of the greatest pain, tests and tragedy.

EXERCISE

This information is life changing, but I don't just want to data dump on you and give you superfluous information. I want you to get real results in your life. As Bruce Lee used to say: "Knowing is not enough, we must apply. Willing is not enough, we must do." How long can you really know something without doing it, before you no longer know it, you know? So we need to habituate at the unconscious level the practicing of gratitude. How do we habituate it at the unconscious? The same way that we master and create unconscious competence with any skill, through repetition. In the book *The Brain That Changes Itself* by Norman Doidge he talks about neuroplasticity and how the brain can literally rewire itself through conscious intent. For example: how did you learn the times tables at school? You remember, don't you? 3 x 3 is? 9 right. 6 x 6 is? 36 yes. 13 x 13 is … hmm they didn't teach us that one. We learnt these through neuroplasticity, conscious intent and repetition, until it was ingrained at the unconscious level and now the question itself is a trigger to create a neurological response and give us the answer.

Remember if you do stress a lot, feel overwhelmed, fear, doubt and anxiety or even depression at times, the best and fastest way to get over that is gratitude. By using this exercise daily you can begin to eliminate those unwanted feelings and begin to control them.

The way I created this habit was by using an everyday activity to create a trigger. In NLP they call it anchoring. Where we associate and create a link between an internal state or thought and an external stimulus. So every morning in the shower (the external stimulus) one of the many things I do is ask myself the two previously mentioned questions and spend time contemplating them. What and who am I most grateful for right now? Who do I love and who loves me? Do you have a song that you can think of when you hear it that reminds you of a past experience, perhaps with a lover? Maybe there is a certain smell that reminds you of your mum's cooking? Have you ever been driving down the street, walking, eating or brushing your teeth and a random memory pops into your mind? It's not random at all, something in your external environment has triggered it. The more you learn about these triggers the more you can begin to use them for your own results and success and even direct your own emotions and states.

I want to invite you to think of something you do every day. Shower, brushing your teeth, driving to work, eating, walking the dog. Just pick one, the first experience that pops into your mind right now. And if you are reading this I'm guessing you are serious about creating your dream life and are prepared to take action. Now each day starting from today (or tomorrow I will give you a night to sleep on it) during that experience you are going to create the ritual and the habit of asking yourself the above two questions until it becomes automatic. Then take the time to contemplate them. Within a week or so you will find that you won't need to think about it anymore, the sound of the shower water, the smell of the tooth-paste, the closing of the car door before going to work will instantly trigger it unconsciously and remind you to do it consciously.

If you create this habit and take just one-three minutes a day to do this for the rest of your life this habit will change your life forever. You may not yet realise the importance and power of this one simple exercise but I'm yet to meet a truly fulfilled person that doesn't spend time daily on gratitude.

We all know intellectually that being grateful makes us feel good, and much of this information is probably already known by you, but have you created mastery and unconscious competency from it yet? Create this trigger today, just spend 60 seconds a day for the next seven or so days and it will be set for life. If you are really keen, stop reading this book right now, bookmark this page and go and cool down in the shower, right now.

Stop looking outside for scraps of pleasure or fulfillment, for validation, security, or love – you have a treasure within that is infinitely greater than anything the world can offer.

—Eckhart Tolle

The second key to true fulfilment

Would you like more clarity in your life? Would you like to feel more certain? The first step to any kind of conscious change is awareness. The second key to true fulfilment is awareness. Truly fulfilled people are aware of many things. They are aware we live in two worlds simultaneously. They are aware that between stimulus and response we have a gap, a window of opportunity where we can choose to control our response rather than unconsciously react through conditioning.

Truly fulfilled people are self-aware of their own strengths and weaknesses and also understand that we are not living in a world of reality but rather our own representation of reality. Alfred Korzybski in his book *Science and Sanity* quoted that "the map is not the territory". Meaning that the territory is the environment out there, and the map is our mental and cognitive representation of it. For example, if we look at a chair, the chair itself is the territory, we then absorb the information through our oculomotor nerves and rods and cones in our eyes then represent an image in our mind on the visual cortex. So much so, that if we close our eyes we can easily imagine the chair. The image we see when we close our eyes is the map and not the territory, it is not reality but rather our representation of reality.

The way we reconstruct that map is influenced by many factors, our beliefs, values, past experiences and geology. Therefore the map is not the territory. This is why three people can experience the apparent same experience and tell three completely different versions of the story. Who has it right? Who has it wrong? Exactly, no one.

Being truly aware of this gives us a profound ability to communicate, understand and connect with other people on a much deeper level. Since the effectiveness of your communication is determined by the response in which you get, it goes a long way in understanding that everyone is living and responding or reacting to their maps of reality and since no two people have the same map, no two people are living the exact same reality. Just like no two people see the exact same rainbow, as they view it from different angles and due to refraction from the sun it is technically a different rainbow from a different angle. This may be another belief and concept hard for some people to grasp at first, but search deep down and you will easily understand that this is why sometimes it feels like you are talking with someone and they are on a completely different level. Have you ever experienced that before? It's because they are, or is it because you are?

Truly fulfilled people are aware of what is happening with their finances, health, relationships, psychology and spirituality. And second to most important only to living in the now, is that they are aware that in order to bridge the gap from where they are now to where they want to be they need a plan. They forgive and learn from the past. They plan for the future but they live in the now, making the most of every magical moment, and being grateful for it.

Having had the opportunity to be a personal trainer for over ten years and working with over 5000 individuals to assist them in achieving their health, fitness, nutrition and body transformation goals, I realised that there was a specific process, which is why I believe personal training can be such an effective strategy for incredibly fast results and creating long-term generative change.

I call this process the PT IT process.

The PT process goes like this. Know exactly where you are now and exactly where you want to be and by when. For example, you might currently weigh 100 kilos (220 pounds) but you wish to decrease to 80 kilos. Then you backtrack from there to set smaller goals and targets and track and monitor everything to ensure results. When results aren't happening we make adjustments. We then align your psychology for success, and have someone keep you accountable to do whatever it takes until you achieve it. We have a plan for every step of the way and celebrate and reward you when we achieve them.

This is a powerful strategy we can use for any goal. Imagine ...

Have you ever noticed that truly fulfilled people seem to have an aura about them, a certain smile? It's like they know something you don't? They ooze confidence and certainty. Ever wondered why that is? Well truly fulfilled people are aware that they are completely responsible for everything in their life so they also understand that they can create and shape the future they imagine and choose. They come from a place of expecting things to happen, because they are prepared to do whatever it takes and they start by asking themselves the right question. How do I make it happen? Then they do whatever it takes, communicate with whoever it takes and never quit in the relentless pursuit of their goals and dreams.

Truly fulfilled people come from a place of expectation. As you read this I would like to invite you in on a small exercise. I want to invite you to think of a big goal or dream you want to achieve in the next 12 months, make it so big that if it was the only thing you were to achieve you would feel happy and successful. Now you have an image of that goal or dream I want you to add the feeling of faith and as you imagine that goal or dream notice how you feel about it when you apply faith to it? Did you do it? If you did, how did it make you feel? It feels pretty good right? Positive? BUT there's something missing isn't there?

It's missing certainty. Now let's try it again a little different this time. Firstly quickly stop reading this, look straight up then come back to the page. Did you look up? Okay now I want to invite you to imagine and think about the big goal or dream again that you really want to achieve in the next 12 months. This time however I want you to apply a feeling of expectancy. Notice how you feel about the goal now you are expecting it to happen, when you simply notice, not judge or worry about how you will make it happen, simply just notice how you feel when you apply expectancy to it.

Did you notice the difference? Having faith is crucial, you must have faith, but being positive and having faith alone is not enough. The problem is that we are taught at a young age not to expect things to happen. There is nothing wrong with expecting things to happen when we take full responsibility for ourselves.

The most important part of awareness is to be fully aware of what's happening in the now and at present. Truly fulfilled people see things for how they are but better than they are. Being positive is not enough, you need to be proactive and take action; massive action everyday with consistency. And become better. Start coming from a place of expectation and notice your confidence soar higher than ever before.

One of the most inspiring abilities of truly fulfilled people is to be able to really live in the now, asking ourselves who and what am I grateful for and who do I love and who loves me are a great place to start. However there is a much more effective way that you can use as well as these questions.

I call it lose your mind and come to your senses.

EXERCISE

We are learning machines; the problem is that we learn too fast, not only the good stuff but the junk stuff also. We cannot not think and much of that time is spent evaluating, classifying and even judging. When we spend time in this state of judging, it can "create a lot of turbulence in the mind" as Deepak Chopra suggests. "In the form of internal dialog which means we miss out on accessing pure potentiality." Creativity, inner peace, innovation and 'aha' moments come from when we silent the mind for a moment and just be. Do you ever wish you could go on a holiday from yourself? I know I do!

Have you ever felt stressed, overwhelmed, stuck or like you need a break? This is probably the best exercise I know for calming myself and dealing with it to put a smile as they say back on my dial.

To harness the power of your true potential you need to have moments of silence, for many this can be almost awkward. Take the time each day as of today, to spend just five minutes exiting your mind. You will feel more refreshed and vitalised than a full night's sleep.

Here is how I like to do it:

Sit somewhere as naturalistic as possible, (I go to the beach for 30 minutes each day when the sun is shining) however it can be in your own home. And start to direct your mind by asking yourself these questions:

1. What can I see? Simply notice the colours: blue, red, green, in the room or your environment. No judgment of good or bad, simply notice them. This causes us to go uptime and leave our mind (lose our mind). What objects, beings etc. can you see?
2. What can you hear? Simply notice the sounds. The wind, the trees, insects.
3. What can you feel? Not viscerally, kinaesthetically. Not internally, externally. I can feel the clothes on my skin, breeze on my face, air I'm breathing, my toes touching one another.
4. What can you smell? Food? Grass? Yourself?
5. What can you taste? Maybe it's nothing, maybe you will just notice your saliva building up as you think about it.

It may seem a little airy fairy to some at the beginning, honestly it did to me as well. But stick at it. When you start this your brain will want to stray, it's not used to this kind of uptime focus. You will also begin to notice opportunities in your surrounds that you never noticed before.

If you really want to reap the most from this I have found that the best way to start is by focusing on a point right in front of you. Pick that point and do not move from it. Now as you stay focused on that point, also notice how far to the left you can see without moving your primary focus away from that point. Now whilst staying focused on that point, notice how far to the right you can see. This will assist in calibrating your sensory acuity by activating the cells of the eye that aren't used as much with our tunnel vision and it will create an enhanced level of uptime focus.

Practice this daily, improve your uptime skills and you will not only feel more at ease and more at peace with yourself, more relaxed and more in touch with your creative side, but you will also become more perceptive of others.

The third key to true fulfilment

Do you ever feel stuck in your life, your business, your job or your relationship? If you ever feel stuck it's because you are not growing. I truly believe we are like trees in that way, if we are not growing we are dying.

It's only natural to want to improve, grow and become better and create more abundance in our lives. Which part of your life would you like to improve or grow? You might be a millionaire but your relationship with your family could be better. You could be healthy and even have six-pack abs but your finances could be better. Your family relationships might be amazing but you are struggling financially. You might be doing well financially but you are overweight.

The third key to true fulfilment is Consistent Personal Growth. A massive part of true fulfilment comes from being the best you, you can be and growing each and every day in each and every way. If you are reading this I'm going to go out on a limb and do a mind read that you really could do or be better in some area of your life, your finances, your relationships, your health or career. No matter how happy and successful you are we can always do better.

Some people might say, "well I did my best", but did you really? Besides is your best really your best? If I asked you to get down on the floor and do your best by completing as many push ups as possible, how many would you complete? 10, 20, 50, 100 maybe more if you are fit? Question, is that really your best though? Or is it the standard you've set for yourself? Could you not come back in an hour or even tomorrow and better that? You have something to compare it to now, a standard. And we choose that standard. Are you really giving your best right now and living your life to the fullest in each area of your life? Could you be doing more? We all could right? So what's been stopping you up until now? Nothing exactly.

If you are not happy in any area of your life it's because you are not growing, and I want to, here and now, challenge you to focus on growing and improving in every way, every day you can. If you decide and commit as of right now to focus every day on making small incremental changes and improvements then you will begin to notice a massive compounding effect within the next few months and years, that creates positive exponential changes in your life.

There are many theories on the powers or realms of our life. I believe all the contexts of our experience we call life can be categorised into five realms.

1. **Health:** Specifically referring to your physical health and vitality.
2. **Relationships:** The interactions and people in all levels of your life. Family, friends, colleagues, peers, associates and acquaintances.
3. **Finances:** This involves everything and anything to do with money including business and your career or job.
4. **Psychology:** Our mindset and neurology. Thoughts and the interaction of thoughts between the conscious and unconscious. I have also included emotions, beliefs, values, and other elements that are at the effect end of the thought process.
5. **Spirituality:** Some people believe in religion, some spirituality and some neither of these. I really want to be as open, understanding and respectful of all people with love and kindness here as regardless of our beliefs we all came from the same place, and I believe in universal love and respecting everyone's beliefs. For some this may be religion, for others quantum physics, for some being at one with the universe and others simply their own character traits not explained in any of the above four realms.

Imagine a life where every day without fail you improved in some way with your health, relationships, finances, mindset and character! Imagine where you would be in 12 months, three years, and ten years.

Every morning in the shower I have a ritual of several activities and exercises, as you know one is the gratitude exercise. Another is that I ask myself and answer five simple questions.

EXERCISE

1. **What can I do today to improve my health and wellbeing?** Go to the gym? Drink a green smoothie? Go for a run? Eat seven serves of vegetables? Be sure to term it in the positive and not: "I won't eat chocolate". Maybe it's to get eight hours sleep, or drink three litres of water. Be specific then be sure to back it up with action, set an alarm on your phone, calendar or ask someone to keep you accountable.

2. **What can I do today to improve my relationships?** You might choose a certain person or a certain habit. For example, you might spend the day focusing on listening more to others. A challenge I like is to put a smile on everyone's face that I come into contact with. It might be to follow through on a promise made to your children. It might be to do with your role as a boss or employee. What can you do today to improve your relationships?

3. **What can I do today to improve my finances?** Can I start a budget? Cash flow projection or financial statements? Start saving or investing? Be more frugal and wise with spending?

4. **What can I do today to improve my mindset?** Can you focus on being more positive? Or following one of the mindset principles in this book?

5. **What can I do today to improve my character or spirituality?** Can I practice kindness or patience? Can I be more compassionate or giving?

This may seem like a big task at first but honestly only takes two minutes while you are in the shower. Imagine the morning already. You've done your gratitude exercises and now set up your intention for the day. Most people watch the news, listen to the radio or read the paper. Imagine the difference in the direction and positivity of your day.

There are many ways to learn. I guess we either learn from our own experience or someone else's. Some people say the best way to learn is to do, some say the best way to learn is to teach. I believe learning at the intellectual level, then the neurological level then teaching is definitely the most powerful and effective way for mastery.

For example, if I asked you to get into a 747 jet plane right now and fly it, would you feel comfortable in flying it? Of course not right? (Unless of course you are a pilot, then well, hi there captain). The reason being is that firstly you don't have the intellectual knowledge or theoretical knowledge on how to fly it. Secondly you don't have any experience in actually flying.

When we first start to learn about how to drive a car we first learn the theoretical and pass what we call in Australia our 'learners'. Then once you have passed the theoretical test you can sit your physical test of getting your P plates with an instructor. Then when you have gained unconscious competence you can start a business and charge money to teach people to drive. And the lessons then will more than fascinate you.

The four main vehicles that I have personally used to learn and grow in each of these five areas I believe are the cornerstone of all my success and are as follows:

Theoretical and intellectual knowledge

1) Read the books

Jim Rohn the personal development guru and Tony Robbins very first mentor used to say "work harder on yourself than you do on your job" or your business. And I completely agree, we get so caught up in our job and business that we forget to make time to learn and grow. We put off the important stuff for the urgent. In fact many personal development gurus recommend reading a book a week; what great advice. I never used to be a fan of reading until I was 22. One day I was training a personal training client who told me that he had over 100 residential properties in his portfolio, he even showed me his portfolio. Naturally I was very impressed so I said, "I'm teachable, please will you teach me?" He replied by telling me that if I read a book first, he would take the time to teach me. He brought in a book called *Cash Flow Quadrant* by Robert Kiyosaki, part two in the *Rich Dad Series* and handed it to me. At first I said, "I'm not into reading and don't like books". He said then, "I'm sorry I cannot teach you then". So I decided to open it and start reading, I then continued to read it and finished it the next day. I was hooked. I wanted more. I then went on to read over 500 books on wealth creation, personal development, spirituality, thought leadership, emotional intelligence, autobiographies and more. I truly believe I would not be where I am today without all those books. I'm so grateful for all those lessons and the great teachers that took the time to write those legendary books. How badly do you want success? You are already reading this one so congratulations. That tells me that you are ready for the next level and prepared to do whatever it takes. You are hungry, right?

Here are my top ten books that I strongly recommend everyone reads in no particular order:

- *Think and Grow Rich* by Napoleon Hill
- *Cashflow Quadrant: Rich Dad's Guide to Financial Freedom* by Robert T. Kiyosaki
- *Emotional Intelligence: Why It Can Matter More Than IQ* by Daniel Goleman
- *The Power of Now: A Guide to Spiritual Enlightenment* by Eckhart Tolle
- *The 4-Hour Work Week* by Timothy Ferris
- *The 7 Habits of Highly Effective People: Powerful Lessons in Personal Change* by Stephen R. Covey
- *The Science of Getting Rich* by Wallace D. Wattles
- *The Richest Man in Babylon* by George S. Clason
- *The E-Myth Revisited: Why Most Small Businesses Don't Work and What to Do About It* by Michael E. Gerber
- *Losing My Virginity: How I've Survived, Had Fun, and Made a Fortune Doing Business My Way* by Richard Branson

2) Listen to the audios

In today's world and lifestyle it can sometimes be a challenge to fit in one-two hours a day of reading, so to ensure I get my daily hit of a minimum of one-two hours of personal development a day, when I don't read, I make it up with audiobooks. Sometimes they are even more powerful as you get all the passion, enthusiasm and tones of voice that come with it. I believe it's important that you get a balance of both books and audios. Here is a list of my top eight picks. Many of these I've literally listened to hundreds of times and again wouldn't be where I am today without them, thank you again to all these giants.

- *Personal Power* by Anthony Robbins
- *Get the Edge* by Tony Robbins
- *Lessons in Mastery* by Anthony Robbins
- *Mind Power* by John Kehoe
- *The Seven Spiritual Laws of Success: A Practical Guide to the Fulfilment of Your Dreams* by Deepak Chopra
- *It's Not Over Until You Win: How to Become the Person You Always Wanted to Be No Matter What the Obstacle* by Les Brown
- *How to Have Your Best Year Ever* by Jim Rohn
- *Your Erroneous Zones* by Dr Wayne W. Dyer

3) Attend the courses and seminars

We can read all the books we want and listen to all the audios we can but nothing beats the lessons we get by being in the presence of the guru, coach or mentor. If we listen to audios and read books one-two hours a day then I recommend at the very minimum attending a live course or seminar at least once every 12 weeks. In an ideal world though I would really suggest to those who are serious and willing to attend a live event of some kind every month. Many of these courses and seminars will also be experiential learning, creating a crossover of the intellectual to the neurological to stimulate the conception of a newly formed habit.

Here are a list of my top presenters, courses, seminars and live events to attend:

- Anthony Robbins
- Les Brown
- Dr John Demartini
- T. Harv Eker

- Dr Wayne W. Dyer
- Deepak Chopra
- Brian Tracy
- Jack Canfield
- Nick Vujicic
- Tom Hopkins
- Eric Thomas
- NLP courses and seminars
- Wealth creation and investing events
- Charity fundraisers
- Toastmasters and other platform speaking events
- Live events by the Multi-Level Marketing Company you are involved with

Neurological and experiential knowledge

4) Travel the world

There are many ways to learn hands-on. This book however is about the lessons I've personally had and how I've used them to create my own personal success. And as important as the books, audios, courses and seminars have been for my development and success there is no way in a million years that I could have learned in any of the previous three vehicles what I learned from travelling the world.

Since I have started travelling the world, and in the last 12 months visiting 12 countries alone, I have grown more financially by tripling my income, grown personally and spiritually more than I ever could have imagined, and learned more about myself and the world than everything else combined.

You can read about the Roman Empire online or in any book however, the lessons I learnt from visiting Rome could not be learned in any book. The lessons from travelling to South East Asia have been an incredible part of my personal transformation this year and I might not even be writing this book right now without them. Seeing the wonders of the world, meeting new people with unique cultures, like the Polynesians, does something to our heart and soul. It opens new gateways for deeper understanding than ever before. It stimulates the creative juices in our mind to conceptualise possibilities that we never even dreamed of all whilst we connect with others on this beautiful Earth. This planet, the people and living creatures are so much larger than our own worlds, so much more than just us. When we begin to truly understand this everything seems very important and not important all at the same time.

Follow the principles in this book and travel the world, do it with style, class and a strong economic status and reap the unfathomable rewards that come with travelling the world.

There is only one principle that applies: Life is about fulfilment. If your life isn't fulfilled, your stomach can never supply what's missing.

—Deepak Chopra

The fourth key to true fulfilment

The year before writing this book we were in Brisbane, Australia it was Kailey's birthday; my sweetheart. I had told her earlier in the day to be ready at 5:30pm as we had dinner reservations. At 5:30pm a taxi picked us up to take us to the surprise restaurant. The next minute we had arrived at the airport. Kailey was shocked and confused and asked what was going on. I didn't reply. Then we boarded a plane to go to Sydney in Australia. When we arrived I surprised her with the beautiful 360 Bar and Dining revolving restaurant in the Sydney Tower. We did the limo thing and I also knew there would be fireworks from our view that night. Kailey was so surprised and gobsmacked she was literally speechless with excitement and joy. I truly believe that nothing makes us feel as good or feel as fulfilled as when we give something to someone or assist them in some way that they are literally speechless with gratitude.

I am the eldest of ten children so as you can imagine come Christmas time there are a lot of presents. 32 last year in fact as I love to give each individual their own present. I'm usually the one with a big pile of unopened presents at the end because the joy of watching all the kids and my family open their presents and the looks on their faces warms my heart more than any gift they could give me. I understand it's materialistic, however it's more about what it represents metaphorically.

The fourth key to true fulfilment is Constant Contribution.

Really be honest, what feeling is better than the feeling we get when we give? Not just a present but something you know a person is really grateful for or perhaps cannot return the favour for. It might be a meal, a warm bed, it might be something that literally saves their life. It might be a simple smile. I'm the first to agree that sex feels great, wouldn't you agree? Well usually if you are doing it right. I don't mind a champagne toast or a wine now and then and I love a thrill. However none of these experiences will give us the long-term happiness and fulfilment we all truly seek. If you search your heart I'm sure you will agree.

When you think of something special you have done for someone what's the first thing you think of? Remember how that made you feel? That's right, happy right? If you think about and feel those thoughts and feelings now you can easily relive them and remember just how good they really made you feel.

As a human being with the privilege of living on this beautiful earth I believe we have a responsibility, to leave this world a better place for being here, and focus on what we can control, which is what we can give. Our time, our money, our energy, our talents, our gifts, our happiness, our smile. Can you completely control exactly what you get in life? No of course not, but you can completely control what you can give. As you can only give something you have in the first place, if you have it, you can give it if you choose. This is why I believe financial freedom and leverage is so important so that we can make an even larger impact in the community and society.

When we focus on what we can control, which is what we can give, it empowers us with an increased sense of control of our own life and causes us to take full responsibility of our own outcomes and results in life. When we focus on what we have or are getting, it usually leads to thinking about what we don't have. This can create states of greed, ego, and other less resourceful and disempowering states. Then even when we accumulate stuff we are still not happy anyway.

There is a great quote by Albert Einstein that says, "Try not to become a man of success. Rather become a man of value". I love this quote. When we turn our focus from success (what many people would consider we get/accumulate) to value (what we can offer and give) money problems as well as many other issues in our life seem to disappear. Jim Rohn says, "Don't wish it was easier wish you were better". One you can control one you cannot. Maybe you can influence it but there's a huge difference between influence and control.

In my last business my number one focus was to create a million dollar business. I did it in less than 18 months from scratch with no money down. I was then miserable and I neglected my health, family, friends and romantic life. My focus was on what I could get and it showed. The way I treated my staff, I came across money hungry, it was all about logistics, figures, targets and KPIs. I made many mistakes in that business especially with people because I was focusing on what I could get, not what I could give. Then once I met Kailey she really taught me how to love again and focus on what's really important in life, people, and the earth, giving and creating and leaving a legacy my children will one day be proud of.

When we hear stories of people that are lying on their deathbeds we don't hear of how they wished they had more money, cars, homes or material items. We hear stories of how they wished they spent more time with loved ones, travelled, told their family they loved them more often, ate healthier and perhaps brushed their teeth more.

There are two types of people in this world. The first person is the person lying on their deathbed in tears with all their family gathering around them also in tears. This person is in tears because they were seduced by social conformity and shackled by their own fears. They didn't have the discipline to take action, they procrastinated, made excuses, pointed blame and now they have a lot of regrets and feel that they have unfinished business as they lie there dying not ready to go.

The second type of person is the person lying on their deathbed with a huge smile on their face. All their family are gathering around them in tears and are not sure why they are smiling. They look down at their grandchild and the grandchild looks up and asks, "Why are you smiling?" They reply with, "You know what, I lived life to the max, I made mistakes and took risks, I travelled the world, loved, lived, learned and have created an incredible legacy and have no regrets. I'm now ready to pass the torch to you." I know this is a little morbid but one day you are going to die. You can wait until then, when it's too late, or you can act now. You can turn all your dreams into reality, you can travel the world, create a legacy and spend time with your family. You are at a crossroads right now, and now is the only power you have to act. Will you choose to be the first person with regrets or will you choose to be the second person and live a happy, fulfilling, abundant life? The choice is yours. What choice will you make?

At the end of the day I believe all that really matters when you leave this world is the hearts and lives of the people you have touched, how you treated them, and how you treated Mother Earth. Did you leave this world a better place for being here? When we leave this world we cannot take the material things with us. Will you take the easy road, which will create a hard life, or will you take the hard road, which will create an easy life?

As Jim Rohn talks about, you can live the short-term pain of discipline. The discipline to apply the lessons in this book and live your dream life or you can live the long-term pain of regret when it is too late. Which pain would you prefer?

When you die your hopes and dreams die with you, imagine the hopes and dreams that will die with you if you don't act upon them and more importantly the people's lives you will not impact by holding onto your dreams instead of unleashing them upon the world. The cemetery is not just a place where bodies are buried it's a place where many more dreams are buried. Will your dreams be buried with them? Or will you do something about it?

Why not help people? Why not hundreds, thousands or even millions? What special unique gift do you have to offer the world?

What cause or initiative are you passionate about? You do have it in you to step up and be a real man or a real woman and create a life that people would write about. Not out of ego but out of love, not out of competition but out of creation.

Become inspired and enthusiastic to help others any way you can, it's not a competition, you don't have to help millions and make millions – well unless you want to. You can start today in these three ways below and start living a truly fulfilled life by focusing on giving rather than getting.

EXERCISE

Create a charity plan

Charity is more than just giving money, in fact, money won't solve many personal issues. If you give a poor person money that does not get them off the street, they will probably buy alcohol or drugs, I know I've been there. Investing real time into people and resources is much more likely to actually make a difference. Education and human connection. Charity is about helping others less fortunate or in need that for whatever reason don't have the ability, resources or education to achieve success or make it happen for themselves. My hope for this book is that it inspires people to face adversity and defeat it, then go on to live a phenomenal life. To inspire people to understand no matter what they are going through right now or where they are that this too shall pass, and they can choose to get through it and turn their lives around by achieving any hope or dream their hearts desire.

Step 1. Family

Start by contributing even more to your family. What's something you can do each month and a massive thing each year to surprise them and teach them the true value of giving and charity? Is there something you've been promising or planning for some time and that you have been procrastinating about up until now? Start by having a monthly surprise for your family, not just buying them gifts but creating magical memories. Take them swimming with dolphins, travel, go on that fishing or camping trip you've always promised. Book something now and surprise your family today so you can spend more time with them.

Step 2. Community

How can you assist in making a difference and contributing in your local community? Is there a school, youth, medical facilities, animal shelter or some other way you can help out? Reach out to your local council and governing bodies and discover how you can help out today. You live there don't you? Find one task you can physically help with each month in your local community with people, animals, or the environment and commit your time, money and resources to doing everything in your power to help where you can and do your bit. Always have a project lined up and know what it is. Focus more on time contribution and don't just throw money at it, for money's sake. If it's something you care about then investing your time is a great investment for your health and happiness. Get on the phone today and see how you and your family can get involved.

Step 3. Charitable cause or organisation

What's a cause or initiative you are incredibly passionate about that you can contribute to? For me it's youth. For others it might be mental illness, children or certain medical issues. Pick a cause today and call them right now to see how you can get involved and invest some time and money. Habituate the art and pleasure of giving, start the momentum shift right now. If you need to do some research on the charities you can work with in your area.

Ultimately I would love to inspire you to be ambitious enough and think large enough to decide to start and launch your own charity organisation. Is that something you've dreamed of? Why not think big? What's stopping you?

It's been a long-term dream of mine to launch a charity for youth and next year we are helping Kailey start her own charity to assist with animal welfare across the globe.

Start asking yourself every day, what can I do today within my family to contribute and make a difference? What can I do today in my community to really contribute and make a difference? Thirdly, what can you do today to make a difference in this world, to contribute on a larger scale?

Every morning you have two choices: Continue to sleep with dreams or wake up and chase your dreams. The choice is yours.

—Unknown

There are many inspiring philanthropists of our time that have made a massive impact in this world, but a few that come to my mind first and have inspired me immensely are the following four people.

Mother Teresa

In October 1950, Mother Teresa received permission by the Vatican to start the congregation that eventually came to be known as the Missionaries of Charity. Mother Teresa died in 1997 and the Missionaries of Charity numbered over 4,000, helping thousands of people across the globe – a legacy that will hopefully live on for centuries to come (Biography website).

Nelson Mandela

After spending 27 years in prison, Nelson Mandela was inaugurated as South Africa's first black president on 10 May 1994 at the age of 77. Spending his years as president he completely turned the entire country around economically and peacefully. He changed not just thousands of lives but essentially an entire nation and he inspired the world. Even after his presidency the size of the Nelson Mandela Foundation that he created for kids and schools is awe-inspiring.

I'm a huge fan of Nelson Mandela's and to list all the incredible achievements and contributions needs its own book, which is why I highly recommend you take the time to read his autobiography *Long Walk to Freedom* (*Biography* website).

Will I Am (William Adams)

You probably already know that Will I Am is an international entertainment superstar that has sold 33 million albums worldwide. But did you know he is an incredible philanthropist that contributes on a truly massive scale? I didn't realise until I did some research for this book.

Will I Am is the founder of the i.am.angel foundation. The i.am scholarship provides future leaders and innovators with comprehensive financial assistance to complete post-secondary education. And this is just the beginning. Having given millions of dollars to charity, building a school and being a part of dozens of other charities there's no denying that his impact will be felt for generations and his legacy even longer.

Be sure to check out some of the incredible work he is doing: www.iamangelfoundation.org/

Richard Branson

The website *Look to the Stars* outlines all of Richard Branson's charitable endeavours and achievements. Richard Branson established his first charity, Student Valley Centre, when he was just 17 years old.

In 2007, Branson formed The Elders who are a small, dedicated group of leaders that work together to solve difficult global conflicts. The group includes members such as: Peter Gabriel, Desmond Tutu, Kofi Annan and Jimmy Carter.

Did you know that Branson was the one who persuaded Elton John to sing 'Candle in the Wind' at the funeral of Princess Diana, which raised $40 million for charity?

Branson established Virgin Unite, his own non-profit foundation in 2004, which organises resources from Virgin Group and more, to address difficult social and environmental problems in any way they can. At the core of the foundation is the idea that the only way we can deal with the challenges facing the world today is by changing the way that businesses, government and the social sector work together, by using businesses for the good of the world.

Do the inspiring contributions of these four impactful philanthropists get you thinking about the legacy you wish to leave this world? How will you make a difference? How will you make sure your life was worth more than just that of a single life? How will you contribute? Knowing your purpose and destiny is directly linked to contribution and helping others is by far the most powerful motivator to help you get up and make something of your life.

Now is your time to decide. Now is your time to act. Decide to play a bigger game, help more people, impact more lives and add more meaning to your own life. You are destined for greatness and it is possible. But you must decide to do something about it then act on it. It's time for you to create a legacy.

At the end of our life all that really matters is how we treated Mother Earth and the people on it. Did we leave this world a better place for being here, did we leave it at a profit?

—Jason Grossman

6

BECOME AN ATHLETE OF THE MIND

Sometimes on our journey to achieving our dreams a spanner is thrown in the works; we can either use it to fix the problem or we can smack ourselves in the head with it!

—Jason Grossman

When I was in my mid-20s I started delivering seminars and courses on personal development. I had spent about two years reading hundreds of books and attending dozens of courses and seminars and I thought I was ready. It turns out that apparently I wasn't. We had spent thousands of dollars on hiring a ballroom at a Sheraton Hotel, organised fire eaters and performers and created a free live event. We had over 300 people confirmed the day before the event so we had almost 400 seats set up with all the banners, merchandise and paraphernalia. On the night 30 people showed up to a ballroom with 400 seats and a temporary stage, and almost 12 of them were team members. I was devastated, it really hurt me mentally. I felt like a failure. When I was alone I actually burst into tears because I had so much riding on it and it was a huge flop.

I had learnt the principles in this chapter intellectually but hadn't implemented them efficiently into my own life. Now I look back and know personally that I was not ready. I was too young with too little life experience. The lessons I had from that were life changing. The problem was that I quit. At the time I was engaged and I broke off the engagement. I quit the business and went AWOL.

I really didn't cope with it well and it took me some time to get back on track for my own hopes and dreams. In fact almost four years. That's four years of my life where I wasn't pursuing my dreams. I breached all my values and hurt the people who cared about me most and I was a quitter. When I finally slayed this demon, forgave myself and put it to rest I vowed to never, ever quit on my dreams again, EVER! And I never have. The things that got me back on the horse and creating my dream lifestyle are found in this book. They are found most concentrated in this very chapter. The most powerful tools I believe from this entire book are in fact the ones found in this very chapter. If you learn them intellectually as I did you will do okay, but it's only when you apply them every day in your life that you will truly turn your dreams into a reality by becoming an athlete of the mind.

If you are out of shape physically how do you know? You can see it in the mirror, right? You look in the mirror and can see that you are probably holding more than the ideal amount of body fat, and you know deep down that you need to do some physical exercise. If you are out of shape nutritionally, how do you know? You can feel it, yes? And deep down you truly know that your low energy levels, lethargy and maybe even mood swings are because you are not eating optimally for health.

But how would you know if you are out of shape mentally? Is your mind not a muscle? Can it not be strengthened and sharpened? Of course it is right! So how do we strengthen and sharpen it? Well, increasing our knowledge is a great place to start, but will that alone give us the results we want in our life, as well as the clarity and sharpness we can potentially achieve mentally for greatness?

When I made the decision to put the past behind me and give up crime, drugs and a less than mediocre life, I realised the most challenging yet most important part of me changing was to change the way I think and act. That is why I became obsessed with psychology, NLP and other psychological modalities. This was critical to learn through intellect, then through neurology, then through teaching to take full control of the most powerful tool we have out our disposal; the mind.

The way we sharpen our minds and align our psychology for success is by becoming an athlete of the mind. Sounds like hard work right? Well not really. In the four keys to true fulfilment we talk about becoming better and growing every single day. Reading, listening to audios, attending courses and seminars and travelling are four great ways to learn and open our minds.

Additionally, to achieve our dreams we need to become an athlete of the mind by taking our mental vitamins. Over the past 15 years of studying hundreds of successful people in all areas of life such as sport, entertainment, leadership, business, communication, psychology, NLP, speakers, authors and more. I have noticed that there is something in common with every single one of these super successful people. I wouldn't even call it a secret to success as many know of its power. When you harness the awesome power of what I'm about to share with you, the only way you can truly fail is to quit. In fact, what I'm about to share with you is so powerful, that when you begin to apply these mental vitamins every day to your life, you will start to notice massive changes in your results in any area of life that you apply them to in just days.

The elite have been using these powerful mental vitamins for thousands of years, and you too can begin to start using them every day, achieving incredible results in just days. I personally believe that with the four keys to true fulfilment and these mental vitamins that you may face temporary defeat, but you will never fail. I believe that if you take these mental vitamins every day even others will begin to notice the changes in your life and ask you what your secret is and what you are doing differently.

Have you ever looked up to someone, aspired to be like someone or been inspired by how incredible someone's life is? Or by how well they are doing, how happy they seem to be, how fulfilled or successful they are? There is one main reason and it's these mental vitamins I'm going to share with you right now.

If you choose to start using and applying these mental vitamins every single day, you truly can become powerful beyond measure and achieve anything your heart desires. But you must apply them consistently. You must apply them in conjunction with the four keys to true fulfilment. What are you prepared to do to achieve your dream lifestyle? Are you hungry? Do you have what it takes? I dare you to turn your dreams into a reality and take massive action today!

A man is but the product of his thoughts. What he thinks, he becomes.
—Mahatma Gandhi

Your four powers

How would you like to feel more in control of your life, your dreams and your destiny?

Within our inner world we have four powers. Four things that we have complete control over, and when we focus our energy on these in any problem or experience it will be the fastest way to discovering the solution. In order to win the inner game of life we must understand these four powers and make a conscious choice and effort to use them every day by directing them or they will direct us.

Many people when faced with a problem imposed on us by the outer world, react to the external stimuli through unconscious conditioning. Remember between stimulus and response (experience and our response) we have a window of opportunity to break free from the chains of conditioning and choose our response. We can either be seduced by being lazy and reacting or become more masterful and focus on what we can control to direct our life rather than leaving it up to circumstance and luck.

Most people feel like they are not in control of their life because of the questions they ask themselves like, "why me?" And because they focus on the effect or symptoms (the outer world or problem) rather than the cause and the solution.

By understanding each of your four powers and conditioning yourself to use them consciously will empower you with a new sense of control to create new possibilities and opportunities in your life, opening new doors of enlightenment, emotional control and the results that you want in your life.

Your four powers put you back in the driver's seat of your life rather than feeling like life is happening to you, making you the captain of your own life and master of your destiny. By focusing on your four powers and in every problem you are faced with asking the question, "what can I control and how can I control it using my four powers?" this allows you to grow and be the best you, you can be. You cannot grow or improve without using your four powers, in fact it is specifically your four powers you use to grow, learn, improve, create abundance and even transform your dreams into reality.

Your four powers that you can completely control from your inner world can be remembered in an acronym to be the best you, you can be:

B.E.S.T

Be the BEST you, you can be.

The first personal power you have is:

Behaviour: You completely choose your behaviour. You can completely control it. Wouldn't you agree you can choose to stop what you are doing now and get up and walk, or put the book down or keep reading? This is your choice right? You can choose to wiggle your toe, wave your hand or smile, or don't smile right now, that is fine. These are your choices. The problem is that many of us have conditioned ourselves through experience and other variables to unconsciously react to certain experiences. Example: fight or flight. However I believe the first step in any kind of conscious change is awareness, start becoming aware of the way you react in certain situations and if you are not getting the results you want then change your procedures, change your behaviours and change your responses. Then you will change your results.

Start noticing how you want to react and start taking the time to think consciously about your actions before you take them. This sounds very basic however you will be surprised by how many unsavoury habits you have. Remember you can completely control your behaviour.

Although we can completely control our behaviour, it alone will not give us the results we want long-term. It is great short-term and yes we must change our behaviour indefinitely but the key to changing them long-term lies within the next three personal powers.

The second personal power you have is:
Emotions: Believe it or not although you might feel like you are at the mercy of your emotions, you can direct your mood states and choose to feel them and also intensify them. Daniel Goleman's book *Emotional Intelligence* is a great read and a great starting point on beginning to direct your mood states. You are right that there will be times when you get angry, sad and experience other non-resourceful states but it's not what you feel initially, it's what you choose to do with what you feel that determines how you feel ultimately. It's not a bad thing to feel anger or sadness it's simply our physiological response to things not going the way we would like, and it happens. The key is to begin to understand what they mean to you, then do something about it that creates results in your life that you desire.

What you can do is begin to become aware of what you are feeling right now, and then begin to choose what's next. NLP use a great number of state elicitation tools including sub-modalities and therapeutic patterns. You can keep this very simple though by asking yourself two questions: 1) How can I change my procedures to feel what I want? 2) How can I change my perception to feel what I want? What you focus on you feel. Change your focus and begin to change how you feel. Change your physiology and begin to change how you feel through bio-chemistry.

Again the priority here is starting to take the time to consciously think before you respond.

The third personal power you have is:

Speech: You can choose to say what you want when you want, therefore you can completely control what you say. Some people say, well I can't control what I say, sometimes things just come out. Has there ever been a time you've said something out loud and thought to yourself, wow did I just say that out loud?

We all say stupid things sometimes, don't we? I know I have, many times. Have you ever known someone that just seems to go on and on, and you are like, wow I cannot believe they said that out loud? Winning the inner game of life means mastering and using our four powers with conscious intent. By asking yourself which of my four powers can I focus on changing right now to direct my feelings and outcomes to empower myself with a sense of control and take full responsibility?

If you let conditioning and your mind control you, rather than you controlling your mind it will. This is when you will experience uncomfortable experiences, or if you are tired or in a toxic state you will say things you regret. Maybe now is a good time, to close your mouth for a moment, say it in your head first and notice how it sounds before speaking it out loud. Don't be chained like the baby elephant to your old ways and limiting beliefs, break free from those chains. You can control your speech, if you are really honest with yourself deep down you know this to be true.

The fourth personal power you have is:

Thoughts: The most powerful internal and personal power you have is your thoughts. In quantum physics (stay with me) now the most studied science on the planet surpassing theoretical physics. They believe everything starts in the form of a thought. That means our thoughts are the roots, and even if we change our speech, behaviour and emotions the secret to winning the inner game of life is mastering and directing your thoughts starting with powerful questions.

Think about it, we cannot, not think right? When was the last time you weren't thinking? Donald Trump says, "If you're going to be thinking anything, you might as well think big", and I agree.

They also believe through intensive research that when we think our thoughts emit energy and it literally alters the molecular structure of everything in our surroundings, including ourselves. To discover more on this be sure to watch the documentary *What the Bleep Do We Know!?* Also check out Dr Emoto's work on the water crystal theory, very fascinating and it will change the way you look at life and yourself forever.

Anyway regardless of beliefs there's no denying that thoughts are very powerful and are the starting point, the roots of weeding and cultivating the garden of your mind. Wouldn't you agree that you can choose to think what you want when you want? This is our ultimate power and freedom, the freedom of thought. Everything in our world created by us started with a thought, before it was ever a blueprint or plan, then manifested in its physical form. Everything manmade in your environment right now first started as a thought or idea and then was manifested into its physical form.

When we begin to choose our thoughts and direct our mind that is when we truly begin to win the inner game of life and produce the results we could have only dreamed of up until now.

Although changing your behaviour, emotions and speech are critical in changing your results in life it will only give you short-term results if you don't also focus on directing your thoughts. You need to focus firstly on the roots, the cause. Otherwise you will not achieve the long-term success you are seeking. Our thoughts are what determine our actions, beliefs, values, habits and speech. In order to really win the game of life we need to condition ourselves to think in a certain way, only when we think in a certain way will we be truly fulfilled and successful winning the inner-outer game of life. This is what we will do in this chapter.

Often with problem solving NLP turns to asking two questions. Is it my perceptions (the way I'm thinking about it) or my procedures (my behaviours)? This is a great question when you find you are not getting a result in any area of your life. You can completely control your behaviour by starting to choose your response, or you can react unconsciously based on your past experiences and conditioning.

For beginning to direct your states you can also ask yourself two similar questions. What can I focus on right now to feel the way I want, and how can I change my physiology to feel the way I want. Change your focus and your physiology and you will change your biochemistry and your state. Unfortunately many people use instant pleasures like sex, gambling, alcohol, drugs, shopping and so-called addictions to change their biochemistry and their state. The problem is does that focus on the cause or the symptom? The symptoms right? So it's only a short-lived band-aid solution.

In order to create long-term generative change, we must first become aware of the change we wish to make then focus on the root cause. In the pharmaceutical and medicinal world unfortunately a lot of the focus is on the symptoms and not the cause. We visit the doctor because we have symptoms, let's say a chesty cough. The doctor then does a diagnosis and says you have a chest infection. Then he prescribes you antibiotics to try to fix the symptoms. This is a band-aid fix and won't stop the problem from happening again. Prevention, I believe is always better than cure. If you really want to change something long-term we need to focus on adjusting all four powers each day until it is habituated, anchoring the strategies throughout this chapter and creating unconscious competence.

Another example: if you want to remove a weed from your garden, how do you ensure it never grows back? You pull it from the roots right? The root cause, the reason or why. This chapter is about keeping you accountable to weeding and cultivating the garden of your mind each day. This starts firstly and foremost with your thoughts. If you weed your garden once and don't maintain it, what happens? The weeds grow back right, so what we need to do is ensure we remove the weeds each and every day to cultivate the lush garden of your mind.

In this chapter I'm going to give you some specific examples and strategies you can begin to use to start directing your own mind and winning the inner game of life.

Choose to be the best you, you can be today and start asking yourself: Which of my four powers can I control right now to feel the way I want and get the results I wish for? Instead of focusing out there and the problem, turn your focus internally to ask yourself what do I need to think, focus on, say, do or change that I can control? This is the ultimate sensation of control and empowerment. Take the time each day from now on to decide to think before you act or speak. Become kinder, more patient, loving, compassionate, giving, a better listener. All these qualities improve by focusing on your four powers.

Mind cycles

So you've read the four powers and can understand easily that you can choose to say, think and do what you want when you want. Yes there will be consequences, for every action there is an equal reaction. However it is still a choice you can make. In order to fully direct your four powers and become an athlete of the mind you need to understand basic mind cycles and how they work. By understanding how our own mind cycles work we can begin to focus on the cause and the roots to ensure we do get the results we want in life. If you have ever tried and failed it is because of these mind cycles. If you've ever given it your best and it hasn't worked it's because of these mind cycles. If you've ever achieved incredible results or success it's because of these mind cycles. The difference is after this chapter you will know how to direct these mind cycles to get the results you desire from life.

The super successful have mastered this unconsciously and some don't even know it. Imagine if you could completely direct your mind and results in your life to achieve anything you could possibly think of, would that be useful? Imagine if you understood how your mind worked so deeply that you knew exactly what to do to get what you want, when you want it. You might be thinking, well I don't want to take a look under that rug Jason, I don't want to see what's going on in my mind, I'm afraid it will create pain, or I just simply do not want to know. You are right, it might do, but only at first. I'm sure you are reading this book for a reason, are you not?

It's like people that say they want to get rich, I ask them, do they have a budget, and they say no, I don't want to see all the expenses and debt I'm in. We need that awareness to learn and grow. We must first admit we have financial cancer and we need to make some changes.

Whether you know about them or believe in them or not they are happening nonetheless. We are creatures of habit and we all have cognitive patterns. By understanding these mind cycles, instead of being at the mercy of our emotions and feeling out of control and like everything is hopeless, it will empower you with the ability to shape your destiny with razor sharp precision and achieve your desired goals with ease.

Thoughts

Everything starts in the form of a thought. We think and then we think about our thoughts. We think in either questions, statements or answers. They are the three types of thoughts. Thoughts are also either temporal or a-temporal, meaning they are time-related or not. For example a memory of a birthday is temporal, because it is associated with a certain time. Whereas creating a thought of an image of a cat is a-temporal as it can be completely isolated from anything to do with time.

We can remember the past, absorb the present or imagine the future. Many believe imagination is the most powerful place to spend a majority of our thoughts and most resourceful. The realm of unlimited possibilities is very exciting. It doesn't take too long to get juiced about a birthday, a travel experience or something else to be extremely excited about in the future.

When we think (primary thoughts) we then think about our thoughts (meta-thoughts) and sometimes we can do recursive loops going back and forth using redundant thinking. This is why we can sometimes get stuck in a problem. We use circular thinking, thinking about our thoughts and doing never ending loops within the problem. We need to exit the never ending loop of the problem in one straight line across the diameter of the loop and break free with linear thinking of a mind cycle. This causes us to exit the problem, think about the not-problem and discover the solution to any problem. I know this can be a little confusing, so read the previous paragraph back again, even if it takes a few times. Most learning takes place at the unconscious anyway. Remember the state of confusion means you are about to learn something.

Feelings

So everything starts in the form of a thought, we then think about our thoughts, and those meta-thoughts will determine how we feel. I know there is a lot of jargon here but stay with me. And besides isn't this fascinating? So our thoughts literally determine how we feel. At first we want to disagree with this statement as it seems too simple and easy, but here is some proof.

As you read this I want to invite you to remember a time or experience you had with a family member that is one of the happiest memories of your life. Now as you think of that time, or the first happy memory that pops into your head right now, I want you to notice, when you start to ask yourself: what can I see, what can I hear and what can I feel? And then you begin to relive the emotions and experiences. Granted it might not be as vivid or intense as living the actual experience, but you can begin to feel it, can you not? If not take a moment to put the book down close your eyes and do the exercise with full concentration until you do.

So if we can control what we think and direct our thoughts, and our thoughts lead to our feelings, we can therefore focus on the root cause of all results in our life by choosing our thoughts.

The key to directing our emotions is directing our focus and thoughts. What we focus on we feel. If you walk into a party and you look in the left corner and there is a fight going on you might leave that party feeling disappointed or angry and believing it was a terrible party. However if you walked into that same party and instead looked to the right corner instead of the left corner, you could have seen a bunch of people on a dance floor dancing merrily and happily, and you would have thought and felt something different again. What we focus on we feel. And we can choose our focus. Therefore we can direct our feelings. Unfortunately many of us do not take the time to direct our focus through asking ourselves quality questions so therefore we let our emotions direct us.

The quality of our life is determined by the quality of questions we ask ourselves. If you are not getting the answer you seek the problem is usually that you look for a different answer by asking the same question. But which is the cause and which is the effect? The question is the cause, correct? So in order to get the answer you seek you must ask a different question. This is why coaching is so helpful, coaches are masters at asking the right questions.

Actions

If our thoughts determine how we feel, then how we feel determines our actions. Has there ever been a time when you've heard a baby crying, a vacuum cleaner or someone tapping a pen incessantly and it just really, really annoyed you? Has there also been a time when you've experienced any of these or similar experiences yet they didn't faze you in the slightest?

Have you ever wondered why that is? Why sometimes you succeed with your actions and sometimes you fail with the SAME action? Why sometimes you just seem to snap at a trivial unimportant thing? What determines our actions is how we feel. If we are already angry then what we say or do next is going to be very different to if we are happy.

Have you ever heard the saying: "I got out of bed on the wrong side this morning"? Is there really a wrong side? Then the rest of the day just seems to get worse. The quality of sleep, dreams, hydration and other factors can also play a big part in how you feel when you awaken, which we will discuss in a later chapter.

If you direct your thoughts you can create more resourceful states and then take more productive and effective action. We see it a lot with athletes do we not? Tennis players, golf players and poker players. They even have a name for it in poker On Tilt! Where a poker player's actions are out of character because they are still focusing on losing big on that last hand and feeling frustrated or angry about it. A professional poker player knows it's not the cards you are dealt, it's how you play the hand that leads to you winning the game!

Imagine if you could direct your thoughts, then your states and be in a peak state all day. How would you like to be able to instantly create peak states at any time? The key is your thoughts and the questions you ask yourself!

Outcomes

We first think a thought that determines how we feel which then determines our actions. Of course it's logical that then our actions determine our outcomes. If we overeat we store excess body fat, if we spend frivolously we struggle financially, if we keep self-sabotaging our relationships we end up lonely or alone.

Isn't it time you were truly happy, you had all the money you need, all the relationships and love you desire and to feel healthy and energetic? Start focusing on these mind cycles and become aware of the root thoughts and you will shift from scarcity mindset and experiences to abundance in just weeks.

So you can begin to make the connection now of our thoughts to our outcomes and how important they actually are.

Beliefs

Once we have experienced the thought-feeling-actions-outcomes part of the mind cycle this is where we will begin to form a belief about the whole experience. Unfortunately we look at the most recent, most exposed or most focused on part of the mind cycle, which generally leads to forming a limiting belief.

If we are criticised, neglected or rejected we tend to look at the last actions of us, before experiencing the rejecting and we associate those last actions to the outcome. There is much more to it though, and now we know. Although those actions played a role in the experience, the actions wouldn't have happened without the thoughts and feelings which triggered the actions. This is a powerful process in understanding your own mind for problem solving, influencing and achieving your desired results.

So beliefs which are simply a meta-thought (a confirmation thought about another thought) are usually (not always) formed through experience as a link in a particular individual or series of mind cycle chains. Our own or our interpretation of someone else's experiences will form beliefs at the unconscious level, usually without us even knowing.

I know this is a mouthful to read, it's a mouthful to write. Simply put though, our thoughts are what will ultimately determine our beliefs. Beliefs are stored thoughts at the cellular and unconscious level which determine many of the choices we make in our life. Beliefs are experiential and locked in thoughts that have integrated into our neurology and so we believe they are a part of us and our identity. However has there ever been a time you believed something to be true then you changed or outgrew that belief? I'm guessing you have. The reason is because that link in the chain that makes up the mind cycle (the belief component) was released and that complete mind cycle was broken, creating a new more resourceful mind cycle. They call this collapsing anchors in NLP. What beliefs do you currently have that you were not even aware of that are holding you back from taking action and achieving your dreams?

Values

The deepest part of the mind cycle is our values. Values are simply the things that are most important to us. Our top five values in hierarchical dominance order will usually be the biggest contributing factors to the choices we make in life and how we feel after we make them. It's important to understand like any part of the mind cycle that they are influx and malleable. Our thoughts and these mind cycles will also determine our values, the deepest part of the unconscious some say. Some experts say if we change our thoughts we will change our world, and that alone is enough. Some experts will say that if we change our beliefs that will be enough for long-term success. And others say if we focus on the root causes, our values that will be enough.

I believe that we need to focus on two parts here. Firstly you need to begin as of right now to start taking responsibility for your own mind cycles by consciously thinking in certain contexts and situations about your thoughts and shaping your own mind cycles.

This will give you more of what you want in the future including more congruent beliefs, values, feelings and results.

The second part is that, although changing and directing our thoughts now to shape our future, what about the past and the previous mind cycles that have formed unconscious beliefs and values? How do we deal with them? So secondly and additionally we need to become aware of our beliefs that were formed in the critical period whilst growing up and the limiting beliefs we have now. We also need to become clear on what our values are currently so we can reframe current limiting beliefs, realigning our values so they are more conducive to our desired results in life. All whilst beginning to direct our thoughts.

WOW sounds like a tough job. It really isn't as difficult as it may seem at first, and although they might not know it all, incredibly successful people are doing this either consciously or unconsciously.

Here is what a typical mind cycle might look like:
Thoughts -> Feelings -> Actions -> Outcomes -> Beliefs -> Values

Although the mind cycle will rarely be that simple and linear, it at least gives you a basic visual representation for understanding.

Wow, that was intense wasn't it? Thank you for sticking with me through that intense part of the chapter. Isn't this fascinating though? It will all make more sense as you keep reading the book and apply the elements from this book daily in your life.

Your thoughts and your focus determine how you feel, your feelings determine your behaviour, your behaviour will determine the results you get, the results will determine what you believe then what you believe will determine how you decipher what is most important to you.

Many people suggest that our beliefs and values will determine our thoughts and although yes this is true, those values and beliefs were formed through past mind cycles. In order to break the past mind cycles, reframe the limiting beliefs and realign the incongruent values, we must understand the starting point of our power. The point where we can start to shape and direct our future mind cycles to create the resourceful beliefs and congruent values required for winning the inner-outer game of life.

Here is an example. A young lady decides to surprise her partner with a romantic candlelit dinner. She has spent hours preparing the food (it could be a man either/or), he is due home at 7pm. It's now 7:15pm and she starts to think to herself: Hmm where is he?

Next thing it's 8pm and he's one hour late. Firstly what does she do? Well she starts to think and asks the question, why is he late? Or where is he? She then answers the question in her head and starts to feel. Depending on her past experiences, it will determine what she focuses on. For example if she has had a loved one experience the tragedy of a car accident that might stimulate a thought of a certain kind, whereas if she has had a partner cheat on her before that would stimulate a different thought.

If she thinks about the idea of an accident how will that make her feel? Probably worried, right? If she creates an image in her mind of him cheating on her she might get angry. So she thinks through questions, answers through a meta-thought then that determines how she feels.

Let's say she is worried, what would her next action be? Perhaps call a hospital? What if she was angry, what would her next action be? She might throw all the food in the bin? This action then leads to an outcome of her communicating with the hospital or sitting at the table in tears with a wine because she believes he might be cheating on her.

She thinks he is cheating, she feels angry, and she then throws the food out, and is now sitting in tears drinking a wine. This will now cause her to form a belief. That belief might be something like, 'all men are cheaters', or something similar. That belief will then determine what she values in that context. So in the context of an intimate relationship she might value loyalty and honesty. Does this make sense? Can you see how simple this actually is and how this is happening all the time whether you agree, believe it or not or are consciously aware of it?

So what does all this mean? In layman's terms, your thoughts are the seeds that determine everything that happens in your life. Yes the outer world will influence your life, but it's what you choose to do with it and how you respond through choice (conscious or unconscious) through using your four powers and directing your own mind cycles so you can win the inner game of life. Remember just like poker, it's not the cards you are dealt, as any professional poker player will tell you, it's how you play your hand. If you let your cards in the hole determine how you feel, you will go on tilt and you won't win the hand or play at your peak ability.

Mental vitamins

I know all this can be a little intense at first, but how badly do you want to succeed? Now we have covered your four powers and mind cycles, you might be thinking, that's great Jason but how exactly do I begin to direct my thoughts and what thoughts and questions should I be thinking and asking? In our coaching programs we actually have a complete Mental Vitamins program where we assist you to become aware of your limiting beliefs, incongruent values, fears and toxic habits. Then we show you how to reframe your limiting beliefs, realign your values, overcome and face your fears and create more resourceful habits. Of course a massive part of this is also directing your states and being the master of your own mind cycles. To discover more about our coaching programs simply visit: www.streetstoamillionaire.com

I will be honest, this is easier to teach than do. I understand it's easier to say than do. Well sometimes. It's a never ending process, an ongoing journey to never ending improvement and betterment. Here are five places to start to take control of your mind and achieve the level of success you want. Stop self-sabotage, eliminate fears and become an athlete of the mind with these five mental vitamins. I'm definitely no master or expert, I'm someone who has simply used these strategies for my own success, along with countless others, and you can too. I still make mistakes as too will you, so don't focus on being a perfectionist, focus on being a progressionist.

If you really want to do something, you'll find a way.

If you don't, you'll find an excuse.

—Jim Rohn

Vitamin A – abandon ALL excuses

Sounds pretty simple right? Abandon all excuses? Come on Jason that's so basic, where's the juicy goodness after all that build up?

An athlete of the mind that shapes their own life and destiny, makes no excuses. They take full responsibility for their own life. They understand that everything that happens in their life is because of the choices they make and the actions they take. Their thoughts, fears, beliefs, values and feelings shape their world. Their actions, speech, behaviour and habits are what gives them everything they have in their life.

Not the government, not the economy, not the weather, not their parents. The athlete of the mind that takes vitamin A every day, understands that for everything that happens in our life we have a window of opportunity to decide and choose our response. We don't have to simply react by default. The athlete of the mind understands that we have a response-ability – the ability to choose to respond and shift and control the outcomes in our life every day.

The athlete of the mind lives at cause rather than effect, meaning they understand things don't happen to us, they happen because of us. That we are the cause of everything in our life, we are fully responsible. At first this may be a hard belief to grasp, but the more you think about it, the more you can realise this in fact is very true. When you take full responsibility for everything in your own life, it empowers you with a sense of control and certainty unlike ever before, a knowingness that because you are the captain of the ship, and the master of your life, you truly do paint your own future and completely shape your own destiny.

I understand that the outer world does influence our lives. But it's not the wind that determines our direction in life, it's the set of the sail. We can alter the set of the sail and change directions, but we must choose it. Otherwise we are at the mercy of the wind. Would you rather the wind determine your destination, or take control and set your own sail? Will you keep blaming the wind, or will you learn to set a better sail?

EXERCISE

Start as of right now, whenever there is something that doesn't go the way you want, notice what you say is the reason. Notice if you use the reason (excuse) of it being something outside of you or your body, and if it is I can tell you now it is an excuse. Because nothing outside of you controls you, it influences you as the wind certainly does, but it's your set of the sail that ultimately determines your destination. It's not what happens to you, but rather what you choose to do with what happens to you. You are right that sometimes there are rough seas, there are storms and you might even get shipwrecked, and you cannot control those things. It's not those things that happen that determine what's next, it's what you choose to do about it.

Take control and responsibility for yourself today, eliminate all excuses. Become aware every day when you are using an excuse, because when you do you relinquish all power and control and lose the ability to choose your own path.

You can have excuses or you can have results, the choice is yours.
—Unknown

Vitamin B - become an 'until' person

Become an until person and commit to doing whatever it takes until your dreams become a reality, and you can never truly fail!
—Jason Grossman

An until person doesn't say, "well I gave it my best". An until person doesn't make excuses. An until person does whatever it takes until they achieve their goals. They eliminate the word 'if' and replace it with the word 'when'.

An until person is prepared to do whatever it takes until their dreams become a reality. An until person takes full responsibility for everything in their life.

Have you ever noticed that truly fulfilled, happy and successful people seem to have that cheeky smile, you know the one that oozes confidence? Ever wondered why that is? It's almost like they know something you don't. Well, it's because they are an until person.

When we are young many of us are told not to expect things, things don't come for free. We hear the word 'no' a lot; work hard, go get a job, get an education and don't expect things.

The stonecutter takes a hammer and hits a large stone with great force in the right spot, and ... gets no result. He hits again and again. After possibly hundreds of hits, the stone, finally breaks. The cutter keeps going with the knowledge that he WILL get the desired result. Because he will not stop striking the stone with his hammer, UNTIL it cracks. Some people have characters that have a bit of granite in them. Do you?

> *It's NOT Over Until You Win*
>
> —Les Brown

We've done this exercise once before but I believe repetition is the mother of all skill and this time you will be even better at it and truly grasp its importance.

Let's do a quick exercise just in your mind's eye as you sit there reading. I want you to imagine or think of a big goal or dream that you want to achieve within the next 12 months. Now as you think about that I want you to apply the feeling of faith to that image and notice how it makes you feel? It makes you feel good right? But there's something missing, isn't there? It's missing certainty. Simply having faith and being positive that things will work out is not enough. Now don't get me wrong, faith is critical for success, but alone it is not enough.

This time I want you to imagine that goal, dream or thing you want to achieve again right now, and this time I want you to add the feeling of expectation. Notice how it makes you feel when you think about that goal and expect it to happen. At first there might be some doubt or negative self-talk, but just put that aside for a moment and notice how you feel when you come from a place that expects it to happen. Did you notice the difference? That's right you feel more certain, correct? Applying faith and positivity alone is good but it's missing certainty. Becoming an until person and expecting things to happen because you know you are prepared to do whatever it takes empowers you with a sense of unlimited control.

EXERCISE

Start applying the word 'until' every day into all of your sentences when talking about your future goals and your future dreams. When you visualise your future apply expectation.

On my journey a few years back I came across this incredible poem on persistence and never quitting. I hope this poem motivates and inspires you to keep going no matter how hopeless it seems or how tough it gets, just as it has and continues to do for me:

When things go wrong, as they sometimes will,
When the road you're trudging seems all uphill,
When the funds are low and debts are high,
And you want to smile, but you have to sigh,
When care is pressing you down a bit,
Rest if you must, but don't you quit!

Life is queer with its twists and turns,
As every one of us sometimes learns,
And many a failure turns about,
When he might have won, if he stuck it out;
Don't give up though the pace seems slow–
You may succeed with another blow.

Often the goal is nearer than,
Often the struggler has given up,
When he might have captured the victor's cup,
And he learned to late when the night slipped down,
How close he was to the golden crown.

Success is failure turned inside out–
The silver tint of the clouds of doubt,
And you never can tell how close you are,
It may be near when it seems so far,
So stick to the fight when you're hardest hit–
It's when things seem worst that you must not quit.

—Unknown

Vitamin C – courageously ACT upon your dreams

Courage is going from failure to failure without losing enthusiasm.
—Winston Churchill

When creating your future, your lifestyle design plan, your bucket list, your goals, your dreams and your vision board, you will have doubts. You will feel uncertain at times, and you will have fears. It's only natural, you are about to embark upon a journey you've never experienced before. You are about to step into the unknown and for many the unknown can be scary.

Many people talk about the fear of failure, but what about fear of success?

What if I become rich, will people think less of me?

What if I become famous, will that change me into someone I don't like?

Will I lose loved ones?

Will people ask me for money?

What will it really mean for me?

It's really the fear of the unknown, which many say is the biggest fear of all. You can never really know until you give it a go and you arrive. By aligning and staying true to your values, focusing on adding value and asking what you will give, will find many of these fears dissipate and even completely disappear. Remember that courage isn't the absence of fear; it is having the fear and taking action anyway! Ask yourself does this action help others? Is it with good intention? Am I in alignment with my values?

If yes then you know you are on the right path. Life is more meaningful when you make it about giving and leaving a legacy. Forget about the money and success, focus on gratitude and contribution and feel the fear, doubt and uncertainty melt away. An athlete of the mind feels the fear, then acts anyway. They understand the more they feel the fear and act anyway, that before long the fear itself becomes a trigger to act neurologically. Fear does have its uses, it's there for a reason. When you feel fear and your adrenaline starts pumping and your heart rate increases, it's telling you that you need to get prepared. Get prepared to run. In the context of pursuing your dreams get prepared to learn, act and do whatever it takes.

To start getting into the habit of feeling the fear and acting anyway, put yourself in uncomfortable positions every day, conversations with people that challenge you, something adventurous like skydiving, taking on a project you have no idea about, learning something new. The key here is to become obsessed with new experiences that allow you to become accustomed to feeling uncomfortable or fearful and acting anyway. Then the brain can become even better at creating new neural networks allowing it to become fitter and stronger!

EXERCISE

Every day from today, put yourself in an awkward or unique experience that forces you to feel some form of fear or anxiety and makes you have to act immediately. It could start as something simple like a new drink or food that you've never tasted, a place you've never been, public speaking, or some kind of thrill seeking like bungee jumping. Condition yourself to feel the fear and act anyway and watch your dreams turn into reality.

One of the best examples and stories I have heard of for feeling the fear and having the courage to act anyway is a story of no retreat and the burning of ships. Retreat is easy when you have the option. When we are backed against a wall we have nowhere to go but forward. When we position ourselves in a way we must succeed, then we do! Although I'm a pacifist and believe in peace and don't support war in any way this story has an incredibly powerful metaphoric message to position yourself for success.

In 1519 Hernan Cortes was the leader of a Spanish army with 600 warriors, 11 boats and a little more than a dozen horses. He landed on the land of the Mayans to invade Mexico for its treasures and knew they were outnumbered ten-one. For every warrior they had there were ten Mayans. This is when Cortes yelled out three powerful words: "Burn the boats!"

You would think that this strategy would ensure certain death, as if they needed to retreat there was no way to leave the island. However the command to burn the boats had the opposite effect because the command to burn the boats now meant there were only two choices. Die or win the battle.

We know today, how Cortés' decision to burn his boats panned out. Hernán Cortés became the first man in 600 years to successfully conquer Mexico.

He wasn't the only leader of an army to burn the boats. About a thousand years beforehand, the world's greatest empire builder, Alexander the Great burned his boats upon arrival on the shores of Persia. By burning his boats, Alexander committed his men to victory over the Per-sians, who far outnumbered the Greeks in great numbers just as the Spanish were outnumbered ten-one.

Both Cortes and Alexander understood the power of burning their ships and creating a must win or die scenario to motivate their troops to win. Do you think the Spanish and the Greeks would have won if they didn't burn their ships? Maybe, maybe not. But there's no denying that the troops would definitely have been more motivated and held nothing back in the pursuit to victory.

How can you eradicate the notion of retreating from your dreams in your mind? How can you burn your ships and go all in so no matter how fearful you get, or how much doubt creeps in you will prevail victorious on your quest to living your dreams? When you have no option but to win, when you have no plan B, you must win. When your back is against a wall you have nowhere to go but forward.

In the face of fear, step up and be courageous the key is to not think, but rather act on instinct. Don't listen to the voice inside your head but instead follow your heart. Your heart is what will direct you valiantly in the direction of your dreams regardless of your fears. Courage comes from the heart, ignore that voice inside your head and face your fears with your gut instinct, burn your bridges, remove your back up plans and do as the greatest poker players: GO ALL IN!

I learned that courage was not the absence of fear, but the triumph over it. The brave man is not he who does not feel afraid, but he who conquers that fear.

—Nelson Mandela

Vitamin D – do whatever it takes

A river cuts through rock not because of its power, but its persistence.

—Unknown

An athlete of the mind never quits on their dreams no matter what. Most athletes of the mind have failed more than many and made many more mistakes. They take them on board as lessons not setbacks. An athlete of the mind takes massive action and does whatever it takes while staying true to his or her values and ethics and remaining within the confines of the law. However you will find many will ask for forgiveness, rather than permission within the business or financial world.

I believe it's critical to stay sophisticated, honest and congruent to your values by doing what feels right to you, whatever that may be at the time. Outside of this there are no excuses, no reasons, no person, and no setback that will ever completely stop an athlete of the mind. In their mind there is no failure, only feedback, and the only way to fail is to quit. If you never quit you will never fail, simple!

The athlete of the mind is prepared to get up as early as they need to and go to bed as late as they need to achieve their dreams. The athlete of the mind is relentless in the pursuit of their dreams, with such laser beam focus that no obstacle can cause them to take their eye off the prize. People will pass, loved ones will break their hearts, kids will be born, illness will fall upon them, accidents will happen, economies will fail, governments will change power, snow will fall, droughts will occur, floods will come but they will never, ever take their eyes off the ultimate prize of their dreams, not even for a second. And if they do they go straight back there.

In my last business there was a time that I had to live in my office as I was homeless, but I did not quit. I couldn't afford food and couldn't eat for days on end, but I did not quit. When setting up these current businesses I had glandular fever and was bedridden for months, but I did not quit on my dreams. I worked all day on my laptop and did whatever it took as I had promises to keep to my loved ones.

No matter what tests or adversity you are faced with, a true athlete of the mind never waivers from their dreams and always keeps at least one eye on the prize.

When you want to succeed as bad as you want to breath,
then you'll be successful.

—Eric Thomas

EXERCISE

Write below three things you are prepared to do as of now that you've never done before to dramatically increase your rate of success. i.e. get up two hours earlier, make two hours more a day of phone calls, save an extra $500 a week for investing.

1._____
2._____
3._____

Vitamin E – eliminate negative self-talk and blame

I am two of the most powerful words, for what you put after them shapes your reality.

—Unknown

Quite possibly the quickest and easiest way to get massive changes in the results of our lives is change our self-talk. You cannot stop thinking. You think all day, every day, and if you let it, your mind will wander, it will do as it pleases. It will become lazy, distracted and weak if you let it.

The biggest killer of our dreams is not the economy, our parents or the government, not even where we live. The biggest killer of our dreams is the negative self-talk that stops us in our tracks. The negative self-talk that we use to self-sabotage ourselves or our actions. I'm about to share with you the five most powerful forms of negative self-talk that if you continue to use, you will never, ever, ever achieve your dreams. Even if you do so, it will be short-lived.

Your brain is a muscle that can be strengthened, or weakened. Your mind is also like a garden and what happens to a garden if we let it go? It grows weeds right? If we weed our garden once then let it go, what happens? They grow back, right? So we need to weed the garden of our mind of negative self-talk every day. If we don't the weeds will grow back.

There are many types of weeds, in the garden of our mind. In this book I'm going to cover five of the most devastating weeds that will destroy your garden if you let it. If you choose to begin focusing every day on weeding your garden of the mind of just these five weeds and are not to implement anything else in this book, I'm sure I would be hearing from you very soon about some great success story or something you've achieved in your life due to the positive changes.

Weed 1: the word TRY

Do, or do not, there is no try!

—Yoda – Star Wars.

The word 'try' denotes failure. I 'tried' to quit smoking, I 'tried' to lose weight, I 'tried' to make the relationship work, I 'tried' to eat healthy, and I 'tried' my best to make my dreams a reality.

When you use the word try, it's because you are giving up or stepping back. An athlete of the mind never quits remember, not on their dreams. The more resistance they experience, the harder they push. Persistence beats resistance. Can you ever remember actually using the word try, after you succeeded at something? No, of course not, because you didn't try, you just did it. This is so simple that deep down you probably know that whenever you use the word try it is holding you back, and causes you to take a step back and stop giving 100%.

Completely remove the word try from your vocabulary. And do not replace it with, "I gave it my best", or "I did my best". Did you really? If you gave it your best until you achieved it and did whatever it took then you would have succeeded. Is your best really your best? Could you not do better tomorrow from the lessons? Of course. Eliminate the word try.

Weed 2: the word SHOULD

Have you ever found yourself saying things like, I 'should' go to the gym, I 'should eat healthy', I 'should' save more money, I should, I should, and I should? And you should all over yourself?

When we say we should do something are we motivated to do it? Not at all. And when we feel we should do something then we don't, how do we feel? Guilty right? Is guilt a motivational state? Not at all. Then to make it worse, we create an anchor that triggers a feeling of guilt every time we think about what we should do. Let me explain.

Day 1 – "I should go to the gym" – you don't, then you feel guilty.
Day 2 – "I should go to the gym" – you don't then you feel guilty.
Day 3 – "I should go to the gym" – you don't then you feel guilty.
Day 4 – You simply think about the gym and automatically feel guilty and you don't know why.

Have you ever heard a song come on the radio and it's reminded you of someone or an experience? It's called a trigger, you can use these to your advantage or your own pitfall.

Instead of using the word should from here on in, you are going to replace it with a strong 'must' and 'because'. Example: I must go to the gym because I want to live longer so I can see my grandkids born.

Start replacing 'should' with 'must' today and watch yourself become a huge action taker. This will also help you eliminate procrastination.

Weed 3: the word LIKE

What a weak word really. I would 'like' to achieve my dream lifestyle. I would 'like' to quit smoking. I would 'like' to be financially free. Do you think the word 'like' is compelling and emotionally pulling enough to motivate you to do whatever it takes to achieve your dreams? Definitely not. Instead of saying "I would like to", start saying "I'm going to", today.

Weed 4: the word BUT

The word 'but' is a dream killer. When used in a sentence it negates everything said before it. I would like to go on a date with you 'but', I would like to go to the gym, 'but', I would like to achieve my dreams 'but' I have to put my kids and my family first. I would like to go on a holiday 'but' I can't afford it. I would like to be financially free 'but'.

I understand when we use it, it seems to make sense to us. But all it does is gives you an excuse and a reason not to make it happen. You will also notice when making excuses people use a lot of these words and distinctions together. Kick but in the butt and start moving towards your dreams now. Eliminate all the excuses, use strong compelling words, remember your why and tell yourself you are going to do it no matter what, for your kids, for your family, for your community and most importantly, for yourself.

Weed 5: BLAME

When you think everything is someone else's fault you will suffer a lot. When you realize that everything springs only from yourself, you will learn both peace and joy.

—Dalai Lama

This usually follows 'like' and 'but'. "I would like to eat healthy, but I don't have enough time to prepare my food." Here we are blaming time and we don't even know it. We are blaming something we cannot control. Therefore we relinquish all of our power, responsibility and control, meaning we are the victim and powerless to do anything about it. This reality for many is so far from the truth that it's blinding, and I believe it to be the biggest reason people don't succeed in achieving their dreams next to not knowing their why.

"I would like to spend more time on my business but I need to look after my children." This is a huge one, and I agree family comes first. But don't use them as an excuse and blame them for you not achieving your dreams. You might think this sounds harsh, and at first it will. If you look deep into your soul I know you will find it to be true. Is it really your kids? Could you not get up earlier? Create more financial freedom and free up your time? Find someone to help out with the kids?

I agree family is the most important thing, which is why you must achieve your hopes and dreams, so you can lead by example and show your kids that it is possible and dreams do come true. Imagine the lessons and values they will learn from you when you do.

We usually blame things outside of us, and tie it in with an excuse. "Sorry I'm late for work, the traffic was bad." This is so common. If you had left ten minutes earlier would you have been on time? Of course. Can you control the traffic? No. What you can control is what time you leave. So you are not late because of the traffic, you are late because you didn't leave early enough.

For many this might be hard to grasp at first. When you do, you will start to take full responsibility for everything in your life and become powerful beyond measure, the captain of your own destiny, in charge of directing your path to greatness. You are in control, you are the one.

Blaming usually goes hand in hand with complaining. What's the point in complaining anyway? Does it really get you what you want? If you are honest with yourself does it really, truly make you happy? I challenge you to go just the next seven days without complaining about a thing, and you will begin to notice how happy you feel and how simple life can actually be. If something happens in your life that you cannot control that is influenced by someone else, say, your boss. There is no point complaining about it to your friends and family, they don't want to hear it. Does that really enrich the quality of your relationship with the person you actually care about? Does it productively solve the problem? Instead of complaining to someone else try approaching the person directly in an assertive but kind manner and never say a bad thing about another as it does you no good, nor does it give you what you desire anyway.

Next time you find yourself making an excuse, complaining or blaming something or someone outside of you, stop it immediately. If in the future you are late, or something happens simply say sorry, and don't back it up with an excuse. Take full responsibility for your part in the experience. If someone else does something or is outside of your control approach them directly.

Every time you point the finger of blame at someone you have three pointing straight back at you!

—Unknown

Become an athlete of the mind today

So will you start conditioning your mind and taking all of your mental vitamins daily as of today? Will you begin to weed and cultivate the garden of your mind? Are you prepared to become an athlete of the mind and join the 2% of the elite in this world regardless of race or religion that already have?

Start with one thing at a time, work on it, master it, and then move onto the next. You can become an athlete of the mind, you can turn your dreams into a reality. You can achieve your dream lifestyle no matter where you are in your life right now, but only if you take massive action every day. The key here is consistency and application of all the mental vitamins until you have.

Focus on being the BEST you can and improve every day. Start becoming aware of your thoughts and how they lead to your feelings, actions and outcomes. Start practicing each and every day the five mental vitamins to win the inner game. You deserve to win the inner game, and even if you win the outer game you will not feel happy and fulfilled without winning the inner game.

What would it mean for you to win the inner game, take control of your own life, stop self-sabotage and achieve massive success in any area of your life? Start using these principles in this book today and every day for the rest of your life and you will win the inner game and achieve desires beyond your wildest dreams. Unleash the full potential of your mind, a treasure chest of riches to be used to create wealth and abundance in all areas of your life.

Success occurs when your dreams are bigger than your excuses.

—Unknown

7

ACHIEVING FINANCIAL FREEDOM

Money is not the goal. Money has no value.
The value comes from the dreams money helps achieve.

—Robert Kiyosaki

The very first company I ever launched was a health and wellness company. It actually did fairly well in the beginning. I was only in my early 20s and launched this company with my best friend at the time. We had the same interest in personal development, we read the same books and he too was a personal trainer. It seemed to make sense. We had an online supplement superstore, sold weight loss and other packages online, did group training, courses for personal trainers and even had massage therapists working for us. We were wide eyed and bushy tailed and definitely naïve.

The first six months went really well then it hit a plateau. All of a sudden it seemed my business partner and I wanted different things for the business, and it was effecting the business. We couldn't agree on anything and nothing seemed to work anymore. We had put so much into the business and was not paying ourselves from it yet. I dropped right back on my personal training sessions and barely made enough income to pay the bills. I had invested all my savings and had nothing in the bank. When it came time to close the partnership business I had no money and barely enough to pay the bills. I couldn't even afford to close down the company. In the closing of that first failed business I lost my best friend and felt my first defeat in business. He in fact was my only real friend and again I wish I could go back and not have that business tare our relationship apart but it did.

I created a business to create financial freedom but all it did was force me to lose my best friend and put me in debt. This happens sometimes unfortunately. We have to forgive, learn and move on to avoid making the same mistakes. Many a great business men and women will tell you similar stories. Don't let this stop you. Remember why you have a business in the first place. It's to achieve your personal goals in a way that you add value to others. Now the business we run creates more than enough passive and residual income to travel the world non-stop and live our dream life. And we do that by helping others do the same. You can too.

How would you like to stop living week to week within the next four weeks? Have you ever struggled to pay your bills? Found yourself just getting by? Or maybe you are doing well financially but would still like even more financial freedom and abundance? Have you found yourself having too much month left at the end of your money? Or maybe you just work really hard at exchanging your time for money and lack balance.

Up until the age of around 30 to be honest I was terrible with money, in fact I still have a long way to go. Everything we have in life is based on the beliefs we hold, and money is no different. Unfortunately many of us have scarcity frames around money and limiting beliefs. How many of these sayings can you remember growing up from your parents? "Money doesn't grow on trees." "Do you think I'm made of money?" "If you want some money go get a job." "If you want to make money or a living you've got to work hard." "Money doesn't come easy." "We can't afford that." The list goes on.

When growing up especially in what's known as the critical period as a child we are highly suggestible and pick up many of the beliefs by the biggest influencers in our life. Parents, family, peers, teachers and other relationships. Often these beliefs will stay global beliefs for the rest of our life, without us even realising the impact they have. When I was 28 I realised something very interesting. That I was very good at making money, up to almost $30,000 in a week, however I was even better at spending it. Then I remembered something. When I was young my mum didn't work and every fortnight she would get her pay cheque from the government. As I was the eldest she would often take me shopping with her to buy the groceries and other necessities. Almost every time she would spend until there was nothing or close to nothing left.

We would have plenty of food the first few days and provisions during that first week then it would get really tough and scarce into the second week. I realised I had unconsciously picked up this belief and behaviour and would find ways to spend all my money no matter how much I made every week. It's almost like I had to find something to do with my money.

I would always run out of money and look at solving the problem by making more money. Have you ever been guilty of this? Can you think of any beliefs or behaviours of your parents you unconsciously picked up? How are they holding you back from achieving true financial freedom? In our coaching program we use specific techniques to assist you in uncovering any limiting beliefs, self-sabotage habits, fears or incongruent values to increase your financial thermostat and naturally create financial freedom with much more ease.

I'm sure you are wondering how you will fuel the financial fire necessary to travel, tick off your bucket list and pursue the passions you truly desire. In this chapter I'm going to share with you the exact financial philosophy we have personally used to create true financial freedom no matter what your current cash flow or net worth is, and to stop living week to week.

I can recall my memories of financial hardship. Most of us go through it at some stage. I recall one time being so broke that all we had in the house was flour. So I mixed the flour with water and made damper. We ate the damper for almost a week before we could afford food. The second time I was living in the streets I would beg for money just to be able to eat. Although I would spend most of it on alcohol. Times can be tough, but you can make a choice. To do something about it and say NO MORE!

It wasn't until I decided enough was enough and I was not going to settle for being poor anymore, did I start to choose to do something about it. You see being poor is a choice, so is being rich. It's a hard belief to believe however it is true, only when you form this belief will you take responsibility for your own finances.

Before we go further, would you like to know the number one secret in creating true financial freedom? The one habit that if you adopt right now you will never have to worry about money ever again?

It's really simple, the number one secret to getting ahead financially and creating abundance in your economic life is: to spend LESS money than you earn, every week for the rest of your life. Sounds simple right?

Many people (myself included) focus on a never ending attempt to continuously make more and more money in a futile attempt to solve our money problems. We make more and we spend more, we make more and we spend more and the cycle continues.

To be financially free or independent you do not need to be a millionaire nor do you need to be incredibly rich, you simply need to create enough residual income to cover your expenses. Then you can increase your means and quality of living. For example, when we were travelling non-stop it would cost us around $5000 a week for airfares, accommodation and other expenses. We had this covered by residual income. Whether we work or not we still have that covered every week for the rest of our lives. Can you imagine a life like that? It is possible. And I will show you how in this chapter.

I remember once hearing Tony Robbins say that our income or net worth is in direct relationship to our contribution to society, the more we give the more we receive, the more we receive the more in turn we can give back. Creating financial freedom is not about getting, it's not about accumulation. It's about possibilities and opportunities. Opportunities to help others and help their dreams come true as we make ours come true. We don't need to be financially free, but wouldn't you agree it would eliminate a lot of stress from your life? Zig Ziglar used to say that, "Money isn't the most important thing in life, but it's reasonably close to oxygen on the 'gotta have it' scale." You deserve freedom, you deserve to have the opportunity to create magical memories and travel the world with your loved ones. And you have the power to help others do the same.

Most people think of money as a tool to get stuff, this is why they are broke. They spend their money on things that depreciate over time. Living week to week or pay check to pay check. Wealthy mindset people believe money is a tool to add value. They use it to add value to their own life by creating magical memories through travel and their bucket list, which help strengthen the relationships they have with their loved ones. They also use their money to invest rather than buy items that depreciate, to have their money make them more money. They then use that money made from their investments to add value to other people's lives through philanthropy and charity. Imagine the impact you can make in your own life as well as others by creating financial freedom.

To achieve true financial freedom though let's first look at what that really means.

I believe there are three main levels of financial freedom:

Level 1) financial security
Financial security is when you have created enough residual or passive income to cover all your share of the living expenses in your household. I have found with most people this is between $500-$1000 give or take. All you need to do to reach the first level is to create $1000 a week roughly from residual income and you would never have to work to live again. Imagine that? Honestly it's really not that hard to do either, if you have the right plan and strategies.

Level 2) financial independence
Once you have created enough residual income to cover your living expenses giving you financial security, the next step is to

create your independence by generating enough residual or passive income (money you get paid whether you work or not) to pursue your dream lifestyle. If I was to give you $2000 a week and you didn't have to work what would you do with your time? Sure at first you may go on a holiday or lie on a beach, but after a few months or a year that will get boring. What is your passion? What would you do? That is your dream lifestyle.

For most people this amount is around $5000 a week. Give or take. You could travel the world non-stop with that.

Level 3) true financial freedom

So you have created enough residual income to cover your living expenses and to pursue your dream lifestyle. Now we want to hedge your income and cash flow with net worth. Notice we have focused on cash flow before net worth. Because it's forecasted residual cash flow that will free up your time.

Once you have reached the second level of financial freedom you can begin to fuel your financial freedom accounts, which we will cover in this chapter, and grow your net worth to a point where if you lost your income you would still not have to work. This is a hedging strategy to ensure that no matter what, you will stay financially free. Imagine if you were to go bankrupt but would still never have to work again? It's possible, we have done it and you can too.

. For many people this is anywhere between $1,000,000 – $5,000,000 net worth. It may seem like a lot now, but I'm here to tell you it's not just possible, but by using the strategies in this chapter, highly possible.

In this book we will focus primarily on the first two levels of financial freedom and how to achieve them no matter where you are right now.

My definition of financial freedom starting from the beginning is to earn enough passive income (income you receive regularly whether you work or not) to cover the living expenses of your dream lifestyle. For some that might be $1000 a week, while for others that might be $10,000 a week. For example, we have a $5000 a week travel budget at present that is completely covered from our passive or residual income streams. Imagine a life where you could earn $1000-$5000 a week passively or through residual income? What would that mean for you and your family? How would you spend that time?

You might be asking the question, "Well how do I do this?" I'm going to show you exactly how in this chapter so stay tuned. The very first step is to create enough passive income to at least cover your living expenses, which technically means you will never have to work again.

So let's work that out, shall we? Simply write down the answer to these questions:

1) How much in total is my weekly living expenses? (If you have a partner determine your share) $_____

2) How much passive income would I need each week to cover the cost of my dream lifestyle each week? (This doesn't have to be right or wrong, just a finite target you can aim for now) $_____

These numbers above are your target. The first target is to get you to a point where you are earning enough passive income to cover the cost of all your living expenses in the first number. Then we turn our focus to the second target and life really gets fun.

I personally believe 80% of a result is simply being aware of exactly what you want, and why you want it. So let's revisit a few questions. At this stage you might have some doubt in your mind that you can make these figures happen, there might be fear, uncertainty, and worry. That's okay, remember that's totally natural, besides this is your first time right? That's why I am here to guide you each step of the way. If you read this entire book, and follow the steps 100% you will overcome those fears, and achieve incredible results in all areas of your life.

My definition of financial freedom and an amount is:

_____

_____

_____

(Be sure to use sensory data terms like 'looks like', 'sounds like', 'feels like' and more importantly word it in a way you can show someone else you've achieved it and it's tangible)

Why is it so important for me to achieve financial freedom?

_____

_____

_____

What would it really mean for me if I was to achieve true financial freedom?

_____

_____

On a scale of 1-10, with 10 being the most, how important is it that I achieve financial freedom?

_____

How will I feel when if in 6-12 months from now I'm still exactly where I am right now?
(Remember to make it as painful as possible)

_____

_____

How will I feel if I take the necessary action and do achieve financial freedom?
(Remember to make it as pleasurable as possible)

_____

_____

If I keep doing what I have been doing up until now, am I guaranteed to achieve financial freedom in the near future? Y/N

_____

What am I going to do about it?

_____
_____
_____
_____
_____

Now that you are aware of your why and you're what, let's determine the how. How do we begin to create residual income and how do we develop a financial freedom plan?

If you speak to almost anyone who has achieved any level of financial success you might be surprised to find out that they in fact use many bank accounts. Why would they do this? Several reasons. Firstly, they usually have multiple income streams and secondly, so they can have awareness of what exactly is happening with the different income streams. If you had three businesses would you not have three business bank accounts? And if you had three businesses how many tax returns would you need to do? Three right. So you want to do the same for your bank accounts. Of course mainly for accounting purposes, but also because you can have clarity on what is going where. Imagine if you knew exactly how much you were going to earn each week for the next 12 weeks, would that allow you to sleep better at night? What about if you knew your exact expenses for the next 12 weeks then stuck to them? By having multiple bank accounts we can clearly create an individual plan for all the financial aspects of our economic life.

Here is the financial philosophy we personally use and share with thousands to stop living week to week and create financial freedom. If you choose to action this plan completely you too will stop living week to week within the next four weeks and start creating residual income. How badly do you want it? Many people will read this and not action it, some will read this and create the plan and set up the accounts, but never create the habit and follow through. Some people, the special ones committed to a dream lifestyle, will stick to this philosophy 100% and create their dream lifestyle. Who will you be?

Included below are the seven bank accounts we strongly suggest you set up today. It's important to understand it's not just the amounts, or percentages, as we understand it can change for everyone. What is important is that you go out today, create the bank accounts and start habituating your financial freedom plan.

Here is an outline of the seven bank accounts and how to use them.

There is no such thing as a really rich victim. You can be a victim or you can be rich, but you can't be both.

—T. Harv Eker

Bank Account 1: Business Account 20% of your Income

If you don't yet have a business of some description it will be very difficult to create financial freedom. I'm not saying quit your job if you have a job, however we have offered two resources for you to start creating residual income below, if you follow the steps you too can create financial freedom.

If you do have a business already, using this financial philosophy I suggest using no more than 20% of the business's gross income for business expenses. I understand there are many different business models, and you may even have a company. The same principle applies whether you have one business, three business or a company. It's 20% total of all the businesses or company combined. If you have a business with staff or contractors I understand expenses can be higher, this is a starting point and recommendation.

If you don't yet have a business and you make the intelligent decision to start using the residual income stream resources below, you will find in fact it will usually be much lower than 20%.

I have been asked many times about using a business credit card. If you are serious about creating financial freedom, which I'm guessing you are or you wouldn't be reading this, my recommendation is to cut up your credit card right now. Why do you need it? Why have a resource that when you are already struggling or not living financially the way you want that can hold you back and get you in more debt? You can use a debit card instead, you will avoid temptation and not get yourself in more debt. A debit card allows you to order and book things over the phone or online if you need to, and can be used as a credit card. If you truly desire financial freedom and are still living week to week, pull out that credit card right now and cut it in half, it's only doing you more damage. If you are reading this going, no way will I cut up my credit card, that's who I normally find out has the most debt or money owing. Yes it might help your credit rating short-term, but the more money owing on your credit card the lower your borrowing capacity to increase your net worth, and the more bad debt you can get into.

Bank Account 2: Everyday Account 40% of your Income

To truly get ahead financially we really want to become frugal in our daily spending. Cigarettes, alcohol and fast food are a good start to eliminate. Buying unnecessary items like clothing, music, movies, games and other low cost items are a great way to get stuck in the rat race of living week to week.

The second bank account you want to have is one you probably already do, but how do you use it? The second bank account is an everyday savings account. Again if you have a credit card linked to your everyday account I would cut it up immediately and replace it with a debit card. If you are a business owner (or when you are a business owner), each week you will transfer 40% of your gross income into an everyday savings account and use it for your living expenses. Utilities, mortgage or rent, food and necessities. We start by living within our means first, then create more cash flow and then increase our level and standard of living. Many have it the other way round.

If you are not yet a business owner then this percentage will probably be higher for the simple fact that your income is probably lower and taxes are paid by your employer. In the case of an employee I would suggest using 60% of your total income for your everyday account.

Again, I understand that this varies a lot depending on your total income, however it's important to remember that it's more about creating the habit of frugality here (spending more wisely and not spending more than your budget).

Bank Account 3: Long-Term Savings 10% of your income

Next we have the long-term savings account. You know the one we all know we should have but don't? Or we do have it but are not disciplined with it. I say throw discipline out the window. Instead, do as I did when I was younger when I would waste so much money. I set up an automated direct debit with my bank, so every Friday the bank would automatically deduct a sum of money from my business account and transfer it into my long-term savings account. I would also hide that account on my netbank so I couldn't even see the account online. Out of sight, out of mind. I call this the law of positioning. Positioning yourself in a way so that you cannot fail. I'm usually pretty disciplined when I've made a choice to create a habit. But if I come home after a long day and I'm hungry, I walk to the fridge and open the door, and staring back at me is an open packet of M&M's, and I look over my shoulder and no one is there, I'm going to reach in and grab a handful of those delicious chocolaty balls of goodness. Then I would probably do what most do, and eat the whole packet. It's really simple, if you don't want to eat the chocolate, why tempt fate, don't buy the chocolate in the first place or have it in the fridge.

This bank account I believe is the easiest and simplest to set up, but usually the first step for most people when creating financial freedom. Habituating not just saving, but spending less than you earn. If you take nothing else from this entire philosophy, and just take this one thing, you will stop living week to week within the next four weeks.

Finally you may be thinking, "well Jason this is great, but I only earn around $500, $300 or even less than that a week". Again, this is not just about the percentages, it's about creating the habit. It's not how much you save, it's that you just save religiously! I was doing a live presentation on this philosophy recently and a young lady announced that she was making less than $500 a week and there was no way she could put aside 10% of savings after living expenses. I replied, "That's great, because that's exactly what this financial freedom plan will help you do."

I asked her, "Could you, this week open the account and deposit just $1 into the account?" Of course she replied with, "Yes!" Then I continued to ask if the following week she could deposit $2, then the following $4, then the following week on week four $8. And of course she replied, "yes". I had her set up that account then explained that that gives us four weeks to implement the rest of the financial freedom plan and start making residual income and increase your income. When we get to the five, six, seven, eight, nine and ten-week mark you will be set financially.

So you see it's not just about the percentage, it's about creating the habit. Get up right now, go to the bank, set up this bank account. Organise a regular automated debit and stop living week to week today. I would love to hear your success stories with this, feel free to message me anytime.

Bank Account 4: GST Offset Account/Tax Account 20% of your income

When you are a business owner you will need to set up a fourth account. The fourth account is to put aside your tax regularly. Depending on your business cash cycle, it will usually be weekly or monthly. The frequency in which your business is paid. The income stream resources in this book will pay you weekly or monthly. For example a personal training business owner could get paid daily, but they set up a direct debit system where they are paid in one lump sum weekly. Therefore you would put your tax aside every week so you don't stress when the taxman comes to you wanting money. A GST Offset Account in Australia is an account that is of high interest and an account you can touch frequently without it negatively impacting your accrued interest. Most countries also have a similar account, so be sure to talk to your accountant and bookkeeper (if you don't have one, now is a good time to get one) to organise your taxes in advance effectively.

Try not to become a man of success but rather try to become a man of value.
—Albert Einstein

Bank Account 5: Charity Account 10% of your income

I believe as a business owner, a citizen of planet earth and as a human being we have a responsibility. That responsibility is to give back. To give back 10% as a thank you for the opportunity to live in a world where we can create our dream lifestyle and we can create financial freedom. People curse their bills, swear at the government and blame the economy for their adversity. Although without these things we would not have the incredible opportunity to create a dream life and help others do the same. It's important to be grateful for what we have and I believe as in the Four Keys to True Fulfilment, life is truly about giving, not getting. How can you get involved with your local community to make a difference? Which cause or initiative are you really passionate about? How can you get on the phone right now and create a formal relationship with a charity or cause and get involved hands-on with fundraising and events? Maybe you wish to do what we are, and start your very own charity organisation. In the meantime, set up a bank account and put aside 10% of your gross income, that way when the time comes where you can do something special for someone, you are in the position to help them out with kindness and generosity. Pay it forward.

Bank Account 6: Travel Account Residual Income Stream Number One

This is where the fun begins. You have created a travel plan and a bucket list as in steps three and four of this book. Well I hope so. If not, now might be a good time to go back and complete them. I'm going to assume that if you are reading this, then you have completed your 26 ultimate bucket list items, your 26 bucket list items for this year and also your travel plan for the next 12 months.

How do we create the financial leverage, and cash flow to enable you to afford all of those magical experiences? We do this with the sixth bank account; the travel account. Many people who struggle with money will say things like: "I can't afford it!" or "when I can afford it!" These are both legitimate statements if you have a poor mindset. Someone with a financially free mindset would ask a question such as: "how can I afford it?"

Instead of living life in reaction and by default, you will begin to choose what you want, then set a plan for its attainment.

As you journey through this paradigm shift to a financially free mindset, you will discover that beyond a maze of fear, doubt and uncertainty, the only real thing that was stopping you, was you. You will begin to feel more confident, and make choices based on what you want in your life, not what you believe has been served to you. It will empower you with a sense of control and certainty unlike ever before. You will feel more motivated to take action every day, and do whatever it takes, because you realise you can actually achieve anything you put your mind to.

To fuel the financial fire necessary for your travel, the first thing you want to do is set up your sixth bank account; your travel account. Once you have your account set up, and know your weekly or monthly target that you need to save that you calculated in the Travel Plan section, we need to get you making some extra money. If I was to say to you that if you were to work for just three-five hours a week (part-time) for the next three-five years, that you would never have to work again, would you be prepared to do it? Of course, right?!

We have helped endless amounts of people in just the first 12 weeks make an extra $1000 a month residual income. That's $12,000 a year for travel. How would you like an extra $12,000 a year to travel in the next three months?

The resource we advise thousands of people to use is to start a part-time Juice Plus business and become a Juice Plus Distributor.

The reason why Kailey and I can afford to travel the world is because we run a part-time Juice Plus business and funnel 100%

off all the monies from Juice Plus into our travel account.

If you keep doing what you have been before reading this book, will you have enough money to travel your travel plan? Probably not. In fact, it's not too long before you can be on $2,000 or even $4000 a month. And remember, it's residual income, which means you get paid that EVERY MONTH for the rest of your life no matter what. You can be just about anywhere in the world to do this. We assist you by adding you to a team with a team leader and weekly online training, help you do events and have an online VIP Group on Facebook for our worldwide team.

For just over $100 you can become a Juice Plus Distributor and start making money within weeks, still working your job or running your business and doing this part-time. How badly do you want to travel and create your dream lifestyle?

I understand you might be dubious, or not excited or not into the idea at all yet, but remember why you are reading this book, and that you are looking for more. Either way, if you would like to travel more and create residual income feel free to see more on our website: www.streetstoamillionaire.com

If you understood residual income, you'd walk through
a brick wall to get it!

—Art Jonak

Bank Account 7: Investment Account Residual Income Stream Number Two

In this book we won't go into depth about investing, however I would like to inspire you to start thinking about not just passive income, and stopping to live week to week. I would like to invite you to start also thinking about net worth and creating the ultimate in financial freedom. How would you like to buy your first home, or even an investment property? Perhaps a second or third investment property? Maybe you want to invest in a business or something else?

I'm going to tell you today that it can be easier than you think.

Many people simply just don't create the residual income streams necessary to fuel their investments first. Poor mindset people spend their money on small stuff like stereos, music, games, alcohol, cigarettes etc. Middle-class mindset people buy big stuff and get into bad debt, a massive home, cars, jet skis, boats etc. A rich mindset person uses their money to create more money and more financial freedom. What do you spend your money on?

Once you have residual income and cash flow coming through, you want to start putting some money aside for investing. I understand you might not know how to, or where to start. For now let's just get you into the habit of putting money aside for the intention of increasing your net worth through investing.

Net worth is simply what you would have if you took all your belongings and sold them, paid off all your bills and debts. What you are left with is your net worth. Although I believe passive income is what creates the financial freedom to pursue our dream lifestyle, net worth is what allows us to play a bigger game, give back to the community, hedge our hard work and leave a legacy for our family with a rock hard foundation.

So the seventh bank account you are going to set up is your investing account. The exercise I'm going to invite you to do now before I share with you the residual income strategy you are going to use is this: If you were to invest in just one thing in the next 12 months what would it be? Most people would say a home or investment property, others might say a business or shares/stocks.

Although our own home is a liability and not an asset, if you don't yet have your first home I would like to invite you to start there and assist you in creating a plan now to buy your first home. If you do already have a home I'm going to suggest a plan for your next investment property.

How would you like to save $25,000 in the next year for a home deposit for your first home or investment property? In a moment I'm going to show you exactly how. Before I do though, what if I could show you a way to save and invest $52,000 a year? That would give you a new investment property and some left over for a small business investment EVERY YEAR! This is not just possible it's very simple. First you need to create the habit to put the excess residual income aside.

The residual income stream we personally use and recommend for fuelling your investment account is to become a VIP Travel Club Member and Representative with World Ventures. Remember in the travel plan section we invited you to become a member? Well, not only can you become a member, you can also make a lot of residual income from being a representative and helping other people create their dream lifestyle as members.

If you are in a serious relationship, have a partner or are married, we suggest doing what Kailey and I have. I have set up Juice Plus in my name and I focus on the Juice Plus and build that business and we have set up World Venture Travel Club in Kailey's name, which is Kailey's main focus. Yes we help each other out as we are a team, however we have our own projects.

We not only save thousands on travel, flights and accommodation, Kailey then also links all the residual income from the World Ventures Travel Club directly into an investing account. Yes Kailey is in charge of the investing as she is the emotional strong and rational one, so it makes sense. Most people in their first year will make at least $25,000 from World Ventures which will go directly into your investing account. Now you each have one additional income stream for fuelling your travel and investments.

Imagine your year if you apply the principles in this book:

- 26 bucket list experiences
- Four trips including one overseas
- A new home/house
- Plus savings in your bank account

WHAT a year...

If I would be given a chance to start all over again, I would choose network marketing.

—Bill Gates

Again, it only takes three-five hours a week, we suggest you do this with your partner and split the workload, working together on your dream lifestyle. If you are single or currently on your own I strongly recommend you choose one and focus all your energy on that one.

To see more about becoming a VIP Travel Club member or representative simply visit: www.streetstoamillionaire.com

If you are reading these and not implementing either of them it makes no real difference to me, but it will make a huge difference to you. You are reading this book for a reason, so if you were to choose one of the options above, which would you choose first? If you are unsure, my question is: what do you feel you are more passionate about, health or travel? If you said health then start with the Juice Plus, perhaps even just start by using the products and learning about them. Or if you are more passionate about travel then you can become a VIP Travel Club member and at least get the massive savings from being a member before you commit to using it as a way of creating financial freedom.

Once you have created the habit, set up the account and are making residual income, then you can get an accountant, planner or other professional to assist you in finding the right investments.

So there are the seven bank accounts. Will you go out now and set them up, start creating the habits, cut up your credit card, stop living week to week, start saving and investing and travelling more? Or will you continue with your old ways? It makes no real difference to me whether you act upon this or not, it does make all the difference in the world to you though.

I understand you may only choose one of the residual incomes or maybe neither. Maybe you already work with another company you are passionate about and that's fine. I've simply offered these two residual income streams as resources for you to use if you choose. Regardless of what you choose, please for your own benefit even if you choose not to, at the very least start applying this bank account strategy and stop living week to week. I would love nothing more than to hear your success stories of creating financial freedom so please start creating the habit right now and feel free to share your success stories online with us anytime.

Get up right now and go to the bank, even if you do nothing else, and set these up, and stop living week to week today.

Here are some examples of scenarios of what a financial freedom planner might look like for a business owner, employee or personal trainer.

Scenario 1: Personal Trainer earning $2000 a week
1. Business bank account – 30% towards business expenses
2. Everyday account – 40% towards everyday living = $800 week
3. GST Offset Tax account – 20% towards tax = $400 week/$20,000 a year
4. Long-Term Savings account – 10% towards savings = $200 week/$10,000 a year
5. Travel account – 100% of Juice Plus Income = $12,000 a year in just the first 12 weeks
6. Investment account – 100% of Travel Club money and/or your Supplement Store income goes into – up to $50,000K a year
7. Charity account – All your detox, eight week body blitz and online sales go into = $10,000 a year

Scenario 2: Business Owner earning $2000 a week
1. Business bank account – 20% towards business expenses
2. Everyday account – 40% towards everyday living = $800 week
3. GST Offset Tax account – 20% towards tax = $400 week/$20,000 a year
4. Long-term savings account – 10% towards savings = $200 week/$10,000 a year
5. Travel account – 100% of Juice Plus Income = $12,000 a year in just the first 12 weeks
6. Investment account – 100% of Travel Club money goes into – up to $50,000K a year
7. Charity account – 10% of your income = $200 week/$10,000 a year

Scenario 3: Employee earning $1000 a week
1. Everyday account – All Job income goes into – 80% towards everyday living = $800 a week
2. Long-term savings account – 10% of job income towards savings = $100 week/$5,200 a year
3. Charity account – 10% of your job income = $100 week/$5,200 a year
4. Business bank account – All your Juice Plus and Travel Club Money originally goes into
5. GST Offset Tax account - 10% of Juice Plus and Travel Club goes into
6. Travel account – 90% of Juice Plus Income = $12,000 a year in just the first 12 weeks
7. Investment account – 90% of Travel Club money goes into – up to $50,000K a year

Have you set up your accounts and actioned your financial freedom plan yet?

If not, what are you waiting for? Get up and do it right now! How badly do you want this?

Here are my additional top 10 tips for creating financial freedom
1. Spend less money each week or month than you earn.
2. Ask yourself how you can spend your money in a way that will make you more money.
3. Cut up your credit card/s.
4. Don't borrow money when you need it and get into bad debt. Borrow money when you can and get into good debt.
5. Track and monitor all your financial reports including your budget, cash flow projections, profit and loss statement and balance sheet every week.
6. Surround yourself with people that earn much more than you do.
7. Have a mentor or coach that has reached the financial level of success you desire.
8. Align yourself with a direct marketing company you are passionate about.

9. Stop exchanging your time for money by relying on your primary income and start creating forecasted residual or passive income.
10. Focus on creating cash flow first then net worth.

In our coaching program we assist people in creating enough residual income to cover their living expenses, then enough to pursue their dream lifestyle and then create net worth through investing. If you would like discover more about this simply visit our website: www.streetstoamillionaire.com

One of the biggest mistakes many business owners make including myself, is not putting aside a sufficient amount of tax. 90% of businesses no longer exist within five years of starting. I believe most people fail because they simply quit, don't have enough cash flow or they have tax issues.

When I started as a contractor (sole trader) personal training in a health club at just 21 I didn't even know the first thing about tax. I didn't know how it worked let alone to put tax aside. Years went by when I was finally contacted by the Taxation Department. I organised my years of taxes with an accountant and was given just 30 days to come up with $30,000 or go bankrupt. I had no savings at the time and although I was making six figures as a personal trainer it was hardly enough to cover it. Lucky for me I was in a relationship with a very loving and caring woman who helped me through that time, for which I will be forever grateful. She loaned me the money and even though our relationship didn't work out I stayed true to my commitment and paid her back every cent.

I'm very happy to say I've never been bankrupt although I've made more financial mistakes than most. If you do have a business, and you are not putting aside tax you could be asking for trouble and a bucket load of unnecessary stress.

There are many people that have inspired me on my journey to creating financial freedom and in business, and one name that comes to mind is a fellow Australian, Brad Sugars. Brad is the creator of the largest business coaching franchise in the world with over 1000 offices worldwide. He is a self-made billionaire and proof that no matter where you come from you can achieve anything you dream of with hard work, a clear plan and strong vision.

I also had the opportunity to see Brad live in Perth, Western Australia a few years back and I loved his direct, assertive no BS approach. He is the author of dozens of books and his business systems truly are world class and another author that I highly recommend looking up.

Another man who comes to mind is someone who personally created one of the best live seminars I've ever been to is T. Harv Eker. The three-day seminar is called 'The Millionaire Mind Intensive'. He also has another brilliant program called 'Master Your Mind' delivered with the help of John Kehoe.

His principles on understanding how your mind works with money as he calls it your money blueprint are ground breaking yet very simple and pragmatic. I highly recommend it to anyone wanting to achieve true financial freedom. Be sure to also checkout his book *Secrets of the Millionaire Mind*. It is life changing!

Thirdly someone that sparked the fire within me many years ago, in which I refer to as the birth of my personal development obsession, is Robert Kiyosaki with his book *Cashflow Quadrant*. After reading this book I went on to read over 500 more books like it and still to this day it is the first book I ever recommend to someone wanting to create financial freedom. Robert talks about the psychology needed to travel from the left side of the quadrant, being the employee or self-employed, and move into the right side, being business and investor. The tools and strategies he shares are ground breaking and reading this book is when I realised the game of money is 80% psychology.

Entrepreneurship is living a few years of your life like most people won't, so you can spend the rest of your life like most people can't!

—Unknown

8

ALKALISE AND ENERGISE YOUR BODY

A dreamer is the weaver of the dream, the dream manifests from thought energy, then is created through the energy of action in its physical form. If the dreamer has no energy to follow through, the dream will die a thought before ever being achieved, and join that person in the graveyard!

—Jason Grossman

Sometimes we subordinate our own health to family, business or other areas of life, and that is what happened to me personally in my last business. I was spending 100 plus hours a week focusing on helping so many people and growing the business that the next thing I knew I was skipping meals and gym sessions and was 118.1kg (260 pounds) and overweight.

In my previous business my number one focus was to create a million dollar business. I would work 100 plus hour weeks and neglected my social life, romantic life, family and even my health. I ended up putting on over 30 kilos (66 pounds) in just months and that led me to getting sick and tired. I was working so long and so hard that I wouldn't make time to prepare meals and go to the gym. I would be on my way home from the office, buy a few pizzas and some Pepsi on the way home and perhaps a bottle or two of wine.

I would then sleep for only four or five hours a night, which led to more food cravings and it became a vicious cycle. I became depressed, sad and unhappy and even though the business was thriving I had never been so depressed in my life.

Has there ever been a time where you have done this? Subordinated your health to your family or your job? People often talk about achieving balance in their life. Balance between family, social life, career, financial and time off. Would you like more balance in your life?

It got so bad one night, I was so upset that I cried myself to sleep and that was the final straw for me. I woke up the next day and had my brother take a photo of me shirtless from behind and when he showed it to me I literally burst into tears. I couldn't believe I had let myself get like that. How could I do that?

That is when I said enough is enough. I made a decision then to do something about it. I was so tired and depressed all the time and wasn't following my own advice. I then started personal training with my brother five times a week to keep my training accountable. I had one of our nutritionists who actually worked at the desk next to me create a meal plan. Then I kept a diary of everything. I created affirmations for creating new habits and kept a mental log and diary of how I was feeling, fluid consumption and sleep.

The whole time keeping the photo that disgusted me in the diary and looking at it daily for motivation. Sometimes in order for us to get motivated enough to do something about it, we need to get disgusted, we need to feel the pain. It's sad but true. It's not just about the aesthetics of looking overweight it's the health issues and emotional baggage that accompanies it. Having excess weight can shorten your life by 20-30 years. Don't you want to see your kids grow up and have kids of their own? Don't you want to have the energy to be a huge part of their life? Besides who wants to be the richest person in the graveyard.

I went on to lose 27 kilos in 26 weeks following my own fitness, nutrition and mindset principles. It was tough but I was prepared to do whatever it took. Once you create the habits and build some momentum it gets much easier. It's like a strong man competition, remember the truck pull? The one where they harness themselves to a truck. They then get down really low and exert 100% of their energy, giving it everything they've got and then very slowly the truck begins to move. As the truck picks up speed the strong man can stand up a little and ease off as the truck keeps moving faster and faster until the strong man can walk easily across the finish line and the truck still keeps going. Results don't multiply they grow exponentially through compounding.

If you have followed the exercises in the previous chapters you will already know that to achieve the lifestyle you dream of. It requires energy. A LOT OF ENERGY! We need emotional, spiritual, intellectual and physical energy. Our why might give us the mental energy, our family might give us the emotional energy, the reading and books might give us the intellectual energy but what about the physical energy?

The key to increasing your energy is what I refer to as the Three Vitality Pillars: your fitness, your nutrition and your mindset. You already know this though, don't you? If you were to create your dream life, wouldn't you want to live as long and prosperous as possible? Wouldn't you like to have enough energy to follow through and enjoy the fruits of your labour?

Have you ever had days where you just feel like lying on the couch, watching movies and eating chocolate, or something like that? Of course we all need a recharge. What if there was a way to keep your energy levels at a peak, at all times?

In this chapter I'm going to share with you exactly how to increase your energy levels naturally and greater than ever before. If you utilise the basic principles within this chapter it will leave you with a newfound sense of invigoration and electrically surging energy, streaming through your entire body like a supercharged long life battery.

Do you ever procrastinate, put things off, or say you will do it later? The more you do this the more you put off achieving your hopes and your dreams. Everything is energy and I believe without the critical ingredient of increased consistent charging energy even if you do manage to be successful and create your dream life you will be so tired you cannot enjoy it and you will be miserable.

Your metabolism

The most important factor in increasing your physical energy is your metabolism. Your metabolism is the rate at which the body uses energy to support all basic functions essential to sustain life, plus all energy requirements for additional activity and digestive processes. In humans, metabolism depends on the digestive and respiratory systems that pass nutrients and oxygen into the blood, which the cardiovascular system circulates throughout the body.

By speeding up and improving the efficiency of your metabolism (in a natural and healthy fashion) you will drastically increase your physical energy.

Hormones and energy

Hormones are the principal regulators of metabolism. There are many hormones and other variables that contribute to metabolism however we will focus on what I refer to as the big seven. There are seven main hormones that when optimised in a certain way will also increase and optimise your energy levels. Keep these optimised and you will keep your energy at peak levels.

Do you ever get tired after lunch or in the middle of the afternoon so you opt for a coffee for a pick me up? Ever wonder why that is? How would you like to feel energetic through the entire day and afternoon? Stick with me now as that's what we are about to cover.

The Big Seven Hormones are:
Leptin
Ghrelin
Insulin
Thyroxin
Testosterone
Growth Hormone
Cortisol

The foods you eat, your physical activity and the way you emote literally determine your hormone production. Your seven big hormones have a huge impact on your energy levels and although I'm not a qualified nutritionist that has a degree that focuses on the information the government want you to believe, I have spent many years studying nutrition, working with nutritionists and helped thousands of people across the globe with their body transformation goals. Trust me when I say that your energy levels are predominantly determined by your seven big hormones, and your seven big hormones are optimised and influenced by your nutrition, fitness and mindset.

I'm going to share with you now some more fascinating information about these big seven, what their basic role is with metabolism and also how you can begin to manipulate them through what I refer to as the Vitality Pillars: Fitness, Nutrition and Mindset.

Leptin

Leptin is a protein that's made in the fat cells, circulates in the bloodstream, and goes to the brain. Leptin is the way your fat cells tell your brain that your energy thermostat is set right and you no longer require food and are not hungry.

If the fat cells are not efficiently releasing leptin into the bloodstream that's when we feel hungry. The problem is that the body doesn't recognise much of the processed foods people eat today as real food so it doesn't stimulate leptin production therefore the brain believes it's still hungry.

We want to keep our leptin production at optimal levels so we don't overeat leading to lethargy and fatigue. Can you remember a time at Christmas or Thanksgiving when you ate too much? How did you feel? That's right, stuffed!

The key to keeping leptin levels optimised is through eating smaller portions more frequently. Especially non-processed foods.

Ghrelin

When you are hungry or thinking about food your gut releases ghrelin. This ghrelin acts as a messenger and goes to the hypothalamus and turns on neuropeptide Y, which increases your appetite and decreases your metabolic burn.

As you can probably guess, when we decrease our levels of leptin by going long periods without food and overeating, it automatically increases the production of ghrelin.

Obviously for survival there needs to be a balance between the two, however we clearly want to keep our leptin levels higher and our ghrelin levels lower.

By eating natural foods straight from the ground in their organic state and not letting ourselves get hungry we can lower our ghrelin levels and keep our energy high.

Insulin

Insulin is a hormone that has profound effects on metabolism. Insulin causes cells in the liver, muscle and fat tissue to take up glucose from the blood, storing it as glycogen in the liver and muscles, and stopping use of fat as an energy source.

Basically when we consume foods high in certain sugars (the exception is fructose found in its natural state in fruit) the more sugar we consume the more insulin is released by the pancreases to assist in reducing blood sugar levels. Again the hormones and metabolism is all about optimisation and balance; each hormone and system plays a vital role. Simply saying keep one high and one low is not sufficient, we must create a balance of optimal levels.

Here we want to avoid huge influxes, increases and decreases of blood sugar levels and instead maintain a steady level.

To optimise insulin levels be sure to consume less processed sugary foods and foods that create a rapid increase or decrease of insulin. This will also keep our leptin levels optimal as well.

Thyroxin

Thyroxin is made by your thyroid gland, a butterfly-shaped gland in your neck. Thyroxin is critical for the function of your body because it regulates metabolism. Remember your metabolism as we know is a measurement of how much energy the different tissues in your body burn.

To optimise thyroxin levels be sure to eat more foods high in iodine like seaweed, sea vegetables, Himalayan salt, cranberries, strawberries and organic navy beans.

Did you know that for every kilo of muscle you have you burn an extra eight calories per hour?

Testosterone

Testosterone is an androgen (a male hormone) that helps sperm production in men, as well as causing and maintaining secondary male sex characteristics such as growth of facial hair and deepening of the voice of boys during puberty. While testosterone is generally considered a male hormone, the ovaries in women also produce small amounts of testosterone, which helps female sexual desire and the maintenance of healthy bones and muscle development.

Testosterone is important for creating increased lean muscle in both men and women and when we increase our lean muscle mass it increases our metabolism. Simply by becoming stronger, everyday tasks become easier and we feel more energetic. I'm a huge fan of strength training for all ages especially since as we get older our hormones slow down, our bones and muscles atrophy and the only real way to keep your joints strong to avoid serious injury is to strengthen the muscles through resistance training.

I've seen strength training help people lose weight, overcome injury, deal with depression, arthritis and that's just the beginning.

Both men and women need to keep their testosterone levels peaked for increased metabolism. So be sure to train heavier and train with a spotter (perhaps a personal trainer), focusing on compound movements and monitor your strength gain and progression. It's never too late to start, I once had a 92-year-old male client who had never done strength training before. I have personally found strength training to be one of the most important factors in my peak energetic states over time. Get to the gym, get a plan and be sure to do at least three days a week of resistance training even if you need to hire an expert, you won't regret it.

Growth hormone

Growth hormone is a protein hormone of about 190 amino acids that is synthesised and secreted by cells in the anterior pituitary. It is a major participant in control of several complex processes, including growth and metabolism. Growth hormone has also been shown to increase lean muscle mass and increase fat transportation of the cells as well.

Growth hormone is at its peak at night in the early part of our sleep, which is why a sufficient amount of sleep is necessary. People often ask me how much sleep is enough, that's like asking how long a piece of string is. Although we know the answer is twice as long as one end to the other, it's different depending on the piece of string.

The common consensus is eight hours, but many experts believe four hours of deep sleep is sufficient, the problem is that you can spend eight hours in bed and not get your minimum of four hours deep sleep. I personally work best on around six hours but that's me. Some people feel they need eight, nine or even ten. One thing is for sure though if we sleep too long it decreases our energy levels. Life is movement, to keep our life energetic we want plenty of movement and activity, sitting behind a desk all day will decrease that.

The key is to find balance here and listen to your body, it's obvious that 4 hours each night is not enough and 12 hours a night for an adult is definitely too much. However sometimes we need to charge. I will often have a few nights of five-six hours then one-two nights of eight-nine hours a week and it works really well for me.

The other way to optimise your GH levels is through HIIT or interval training. GH is peaked when lactic acid is released into the bloodstream. When we do lactate training where the muscles are under tension for an extended period of time we get that burning sensation. You know the one right? Doing 30 minutes on the cross trainer with 30 second sprints every three minutes can be a great way to peak your natural growth hormone production for increased energy, fat loss and lean muscle mass.

Cortisol

Cortisol is an important hormone in the body, secreted by the adrenal glands and involved in proper glucose metabolism, regulation of blood pressure and insulin release for blood and sugar maintenance. It is also the hormone released when we experience stress. Which often leads to it being called the stress hormone. Do you ever feel stressed and tired at the same time? No surprise.

We experience stress everyday: oxidative stress, emotional stress, intellectual stress and pressures of everyday life. When we emote and feel stress it also stimulates an increased production of cortisol. Cortisol can decrease fat transportation and increases fat storage in those problem areas like the midsection.

Adrenal fatigue is an issue with many more people these days and a huge energy drainer. This is why travelling, taking time with your family and for those who really want the dream life, yoga, pilates and meditation can really help you relax and optimise those cortisol levels.

Don't you deserve to be able to relax easily, zone out, simply take a breath and smile? The gratitude exercises and losing your mind exercises in this book are also a great way to optimise your cortisol levels.

If you focus on the basics above by eating smaller portions more frequently, exercising every day (preferably in the morning), taking time out to relax, eating natural organic foods and eliminating processed sugars you will begin to notice a huge increase in your energy levels. If at any stage you find after all of this and the remaining principles in this chapter that you are still low in energy perhaps take the time to see a hormone specialist and have some tests done to see where you are at and what you need to work on.

In the health and fitness industry there is a lot of focus on weight loss and cosmetics. And although I do agree that it is important to be happy with your body, if instead of focusing on counting calories and macronutrients (carbohydrate, protein and fats) you focus on micronutrients and phytonutrients you will find that your body composition will begin to shift and body fat levels decrease.

If you are holding extra body fat (if you are honest with yourself you know if you are) then now is a good time to seek out a professional, have some accountability, have a plan and start looking and feeling the way you truly deserve. Can you really live a long, prosperous life you dream of with all that extra, unwanted fat and without peak energy levels? Take action now, apply these principles and focus on being healthy.

Take care of your body. It's the only place you have to live.

—Jim Rohn

Alkalise and Energise

Do you want to be the richest person in the graveyard? No one really wants that, do they? If you truly are living a dream life that makes you have to pinch yourself daily, wouldn't you want to live as long as possible? To extend your lifespan by 10, 20 or even 30 or more years?

I'm guessing the answer is yes. If you have begun to habituate all the exercises and philosophies in this book, then I'm sure you will agree that you can see more clearly than ever where you are heading in this beautiful life.

Wouldn't you want to live as long as humanly and healthily possible? To see your kids walk down the aisle one day, see your grandkids being born, maybe even growing up? To live and experience the whimsical changes and advancements of our society, technology to travel to as many places and absorb as many unique experiences as possible? If you are living a dream life, every day is a once in a lifetime opportunity, and tomorrow could be one missed.

I believe that the most important ingredient is energy. Everything is energy, even matter. The more energy we have, the better we feel and the more motivated we are to take action and create our dream life. The more energy we have the better we communicate, happier and more positive we are. Has there ever been a day you just wanted to lie on the couch and do nothing? I'm sure there has been. Alternatively, has there ever been a day you were so motivated that your productivity went through the roof? It was like someone put an energy booster in your water. And no I'm not talking about coffee. Imagine having abundant energy every day, living each day like it was your last and taking massive action. To maximise your energy levels we must focus on mind-set, your nutrition and physical fitness.

After almost 15 years in the Health and Wellness industry, learning about exercise science, bio-chemistry, nutrition, mindset, NLP and more, the most profound literature and research I have come across for living a happier, healthier longer life revolves around the process of alkalisation.

A surprising number and variety of physical problems and diseases can be caused by the problem of foods that are acid-producing after digestion. And lifestyle choices that create toxins in the body. Today the vast majority of the populace in industrialised nations suffer from problems caused by the stress of acidosis, because both modern lifestyle and diet promote acidification of the body's internal environment.

The current typical Western diet is largely composed of acid-forming foods (animal proteins, and processed sugars). Alkaline-producing foods such as vegetables are eaten in much smaller quantities. Stimulants like tobacco, coffee, tea and alcohol are also extremely acidifying. Stress and physical activity can also cause acidification.

Many foods are alkaline-producing or neutral by nature, but manufactured processed foods are mostly acid-producing, and these are the ones most heavily advertised in the media and filling the shelves of supermarkets. It is important to consume at least 70-80% alkaline-producing foods in our diet, in order to maintain health. We need plenty of fresh fruits and particularly vegetables (alkaline-producing) to balance our necessary protein intake (acid-producing). And we need to avoid processed and sugary foods, not only because they are acid-producing, but also because they raise blood sugar levels too quickly with high glycaemic index, therefore fattening and stressing our insulin response – plus they tend to be nutrient-lacking and may be toxic too.

The body maintains correct pH in the blood at all costs through homeostasis, but it is stressful for the body's system and resources when the diet is unbalanced in terms of acid-forming foods (the residue after digestion, that is). Within cells it's a different story. Saliva and urine tests show clearly enough the changes in alkalinity or acidity that are caused by diet and lifestyle.

The food you eat can be either the safest and most powerful form of medicine or the slowest form of poison.

—Ann Wigmore

What is the body's pH?

Water is the most abundant compound in the human body, comprising of around 70%. The body therefore contains a wide range of solutions, which may be more or less acidic. pH (potential of Hydrogen) is a measure of the acidity or alkalinity of a solution – the ratio between positively charged ions (acid-forming) and negatively charged ions (alkaline-forming.) The pH of any solution is the measure of its hydrogen-ion concentration. The higher the pH reading, the more alkaline and oxygen rich the fluid is. The lower the pH reading, the more acidic and oxygen deprived the fluid is. The pH range is from 0 to 14, with 7.0 being neutral. Anything above 7.0 is alkaline, anything below 7.0 is considered acidic.

Human blood pH levels should be slightly alkaline (7.35 - 7.45). Below or above this range means symptoms and disease. If blood pH moves below 6.8 or above 7.8, cells stop functioning and the body dies. The body therefore continually strives to balance pH. When this balance is compromised many problems can occur.

An imbalanced diet high in acidic-producing foods such as animal protein, sugar, caffeine, and processed foods puts pressure on the body's regulating systems to maintain pH neutrality. The extra buffering required can deplete the body of alkaline minerals such as sodium, potassium, magnesium and calcium, making the person prone to chronic and degenerative disease.

It's also important to understand that cancer, which currently kills over one-third of our population, can only exist in an environment deprived of oxygen that leads to acidity within the blood and body. When cells are highly oxygenised, cancer can simply not survive, let alone thrive.

By choosing the right foods, it's actually quite easy to eat a diet rich in alkaline-producing foods. Most fresh fruits and vegetables are excellent choices. Red meat is not a good choice, but you can add plenty of protein to your meals by using delicious beans, legumes, and nuts such as almonds. You should eliminate unhealthy fats from your diet, but you can use good fats such as olive oil, avocado and coconut. High fat dairy products should be avoided, but you can drink almond milk as an alternative. Replace the empty calories of soda with delicious iced herb tea, green tea and lemon water. Coffee should be avoided, but you can drink hot herbal or green tea. Replace pasta with healthy whole grains such as wild rice, millet and quinoa. When sweetening your foods, focus on natural products such as Stevia. As you can see, you'll have many nutritious choices that are both delicious and high in alkalising properties.

To maintain a balanced healthy diet you want to select at least 80% of your foods from the alkaline section in the chart on the next page and a maximum of 20% from the acidic. The more you avoid really acidic foods the healthier you will be and more energetic you will feel. Ditch that afternoon coffee and live freely from lethargy. Many people simply don't realise how good being fit and healthy feels because they have never experienced it and don't have anything to compare it to. Of course enjoy a cheeky slice of cheesecake or a glass of wine every now and then, I do. BUT make the majority of your foods and meals alkaline-producing foods and full of life force energy.

Every 35 days, your skin replaces itself. Your liver, about a month.
Your body makes these new cells from the food you eat.
What you eat literally becomes you.

—Unknown

Many people don't realise that 80% or more of ALL illness and sickness in one way or another is caused by our nutrition and over 90% caused by our lifestyle choices of some kind. We stuff our faces with junk food, processed foods, and carbonated drinks then spend huge amounts of money on pills and medication that focus on the symptoms not the cause. Imagine how much money you would save on your family's medical bills if you simply followed the basic nutrition and lifestyle principles in this book.

We've all heard the saying, "an apple a day keeps the doctor away". Did you know that an apple has over 10,000 phytonutrients many of which cannot be found in any other food source on the planet? We literally are what we eat. Every few days the cells of the digestive system are fully renewed and totally new cells are formed. The same happens with your internal organs, skin and the rest of your body. The food and drink we eat creates the building blocks necessary for conception and gestation of the new cells. Simply put, the new cells are literally made up of the nutrients we consume (or lack of). This is a big part of the reason why some people seem to have that healthy glow. Have you ever met someone that just seems to be absolutely glowing? It's because of the nutrients they are consuming. What you eat literally determines what you are made of, how you look and how you feel.

Green vegetables are definitely a great start. In fact I highly recommend at least one-two green smoothies a day. By having it in a smoothie this allows you to compact three-five serves of greens into one consumable drink, with a high nutrient rich value for energising and alkalising. Juicing is also a great option.

Here is a recipe for my favourite easy to make green smoothie:

Jason's Favourite Green Smoothie
- 3 cups of fresh kale
- 1 x celery stalk
- 3 cups of spinach
- ¼ of a cucumber
- 2 x oranges
- 1 x carrot

Place it all in a high speed blender and drink.

At-a-glance Acid/Alkaline Food List

EAT LESS

Highly Acidic	Moderately Acidic	Neutral/ Mildly Acidic
Alcohol	Natural Juice	Black Beans
Coffee & Black Tea		Chickpeas/ Garbanzos
Fruit Juice (sweetened)	Ketchup	Kidney Beans
	Mayonnaise	Seitan
Cacoa	Butter	
Honey		Cantaloupe
Jam	Apple	Currants
Jelly	Apricot	Fresh Dates
Mustard	Banana	Nectarines
Miso	Blackberry	Plum
Rice Syrup	Blueberry	Sweet Cherry
Soy Sauce	Cranberry	Watermelon
Vinegar	Grapes	
Yeast	Mango	Amaranth
	Mangosteen	Millet
Dried Fruit	Orange	Oats/ Oatmeal
	Peach	Spelt
Beef	Papaya	Soybeans
Chicken	Pineapple	
Eggs	Strawberry	Rice/ Soy/ Hemp
Farmed Fish		Protein
Pork	Brown Rice	
Shellfish	Oats	Freshwater Wild Fish
	Rye Bread	
Cheese	Wheat	Rice & Soy Milk
Dairy	Wholemeal Bread	
	Wild Rice	Brazil Nuts
Artificial Sweeteners	Wholemeal Pasta	Pecan Nuts
Syrup		Hazel Nuts
	Ocean Fish	
Mushrooms		Sunflower Oil
		Grapeseed Oil

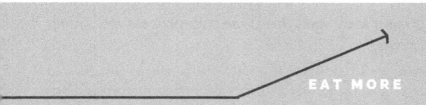

EAT MORE

Mildly Alkaline	Moderately Alkaline	Highly Alkaline
Artichoke	Avocado	pH 9.5 alkaline Water
Asparagus	Beetroot	
Brussels Sprout	Capsicum/ Pepper	Himalayan Salt
Cauliflower	Cabbage	
Carrot	Celery	Grasses
Chives	Collard/ Spring Greens	Cucumber
Courgette/ Zucchini	Endive	Kale
Leaks	Garlic	Kelp
New Baby Potato	Ginger	Spinach
Peas	Green Beans	Parsley
Rhubarb	Lettuce	Broccoli
Swede	Mustard Greens	Sprouts (soy, alfalfa etc)
Watercress	Okra	Sea Vegetables (kelp)
	Onion	
Grapefruit	Radish	Green Drinks
Coconut	Red Onion	
	Rocket/ Arugula	All Sprouted Beans/
Buckwheat	Tomato	Sprouts
Quinoa		
Spelt	Lemon	
Lentils	Lime	
Tofu		
	Butter Beans	
Other Beans & Legumes	Soy Beans	
Goat & Almond Milk	White Haricot Beans	
Most Herbs & Spices	Chia/ Salba	
	Quinoa	
Avocado Oil		
Coconut Oil		
Flax Oil		

How do you kick start the alkalizing process and boost your energy?

Detoxifying your body will fast track the alkalising process and energise your body quickly and effectively. Not only will a detox assist you in realkalising your body causing you to feel more energetic, invigorated, healthier, less bloated and all round happier, it will also assist you in beginning to create new life-enhancing eating habits that will also positively impact the people in your life and family.

What is detoxification?

Well, simply put it's a basic process that intentionally removes as many of the bodies 'unwanted' toxins as possible. Every day we breathe air and eat food that is full of free radicals and toxins, causing our body to go into an acidic state, opening a window to allow for sickness, illness, slow metabolism, bloated-ness and increased body fat!

When the cells are hit with these toxins and free radicals, it literally kills off the electrons, and once the cell reaches a certain amount of electrons then the cell dies. Once the cell dies it is replaced by a weaker version of its former self with less of the receptor sites it wasn't using (i.e. to absorb nutrients), and more of the receptor sites it was using (i.e. fat). So the key is to use nutrients, minerals and antioxidants that are known as methyl-donors to help replenish the electrons at the cellular level. The most powerful way to do this is through increasing the alkalinity in our body.

You can break a habit anytime, but creating a new one may take time. So using a full seven day detox with all the recipes, shopping lists, meal planners, VIP support group and more might just be exactly what you need to create positive eating habits and a much healthier and happier lifestyle. Live longer! Live Stronger! You deserve to feel good and be happy!

If you are serious about living healthier, with more energy and living longer whilst creating your dream lifestyle, you really want to energise and alkalise as soon as possible. You can do that with our very popular global '7 Day Raw Detox Challenge' with tons of recipes and more by visiting this website: www.7dayrawdetox.com

95% of people do NOT consume a sufficient amount of nutrients in the form of at least two-three serves of fruit and seven-nine serves (that's cups) of vegetables a day! How many do you eat? Do you eat 60-70 serves of fruit and vegetables a week? If you are like most people then probably not!

By not consuming enough micro-nutrients and phytonutrients you are at a much larger risk of being diagnosed with cancer, heart-related disease, diabetes and more. Plus by consuming a sufficient amount of nutrients on a regular basis you may even increase your life span by as much as 10-20 years! What would it truly mean to be able to live a happier, healthier life?

Another fast and effective long-term solution is to ensure that you always consume a sufficient amount of micro-nutrients, which is what I do especially when travelling and I use Juice Plus. As we travel a lot sometimes it's hard to eat enough fruit and vegetables. I want to avoid synthetic vitamins and multis so I personally consume Juice Plus to stay healthy, keep lean and peak my energy levels.

Juice Plus is also a great option if you have trouble getting your kids to eat their veggies. You can even get it free for your child between the ages of 4-17. Plus there is a chewable option. Although you cannot beat real food, we highly recommend Juice Plus to ensure you consume enough nutrients every day. To discover more about Juice Plus and its many benefits simply visit: www.streetstoamillionaire.com

An example of an ideal day for maximum energy

In addition to our nutrition with food consumption, it's also vital to drink plenty of fluids and perform regular physical activity. So below I have given an example of an ideal day with food, fluid and exercise. I strongly recommend physical exercise five-six times a week in addition to sport or being active. And have one day a week to relax, enjoy and celebrate life. If you have a stressful job or business, doing regular yoga, Pilates and meditation is highly recommended.

As we understand everyone is different and requires different attention, if you would like any further assistance with meal plans, fitness plans or weight loss you can find all the resources you need on our website: www.fromthestreetstoamillionaire.com

Please note this is just an example and basic suggestion for an ideal day, always seek the advice of an expert with one-on-one consultation to ensure safety and results.

Here is an example of an ideal day:

5:30am:	Wake up and drink 1 litre of filtered water with 1 lemon cut in half and juice squeezed
6am:	1 hour of exercise at least 30 minutes of cardio
8am:	2 cups of fruit salad and 1 x Complete Protein drink
10am:	Green smoothie and Juice Plus
12pm:	Pumpkin and quinoa Salad with green vegetables / salad and seeds
2pm:	500ml-1L coconut water and Juice Plus
5pm:	Thai chicken salad with plenty of greens
8pm:	Complete Protein drink and / or some fresh strawberries / banana

Please note this is simply an example and not a personalised meal plan. It's also important to drink two-three litres of water throughout the day to stay hydrated for maximum energy levels and cleanse the kidneys. So many people are simply tired because they don't drink enough water. It's incredible just how many.

I truly couldn't imagine a life without exercise, without strength training and definitely not without my daily green smoothies. They give me the zest needed for my busy and adventurous lifestyle and the energy to pursue my dreams with incredible intensity and passion.

I believe that life is about balance. Enjoy a glass of champagne, have a chocolate every now and then, but just ensure that the bulk of your nutrition is alkalising and healthy. Make sure you exercise almost every day, and be sure to drink two-three litres of water a day minimum. If you struggle to drink plain water put some lemon in your water, or even do what I do and drink organic coconut water. By simply following all the above steps you can begin to dramatically and exponentially increase your energy levels and feel more alive and invigorated than ever before. You deserve to feel amazing, you deserve to be healthy, and you deserve to enjoy the full rewards that come with living a truly healthy dream lifestyle. Stop feeling tired and lethargic and start really living your life.

You are what you eat, so don't be fast, easy, cheap or fake.

—Unknown

9

7 UNIVERSAL LAWS

Winning the game of life is about understanding that we live in two worlds simultaneously, the inner world and the outer world. We must understand and focus on what we can control, harnessing the four powers of our inner world, as we live harmoniously and succinctly with the laws outside of our control governing the outer world!

—Jason Grossman

Everything in the universe is governed by laws. We know this to be true because as the law of gravity states that any two bodies in the universe attract each other with a force that is directly proportional to the product of their masses and inversely proportional to the square of the distance between them. We know the law of gravity exists which is why we don't go jump off a tall building or bridge (well without a bungee) because we know gravity exists and we will die when we hit the ground, or seriously injure ourselves if we do.

I recall at one stage of my life living with drug dealers. You can expect that there are certain things that are going to happen if you situate yourself in a household like that. We did a lot of drugs there. I had threesomes and meaningless sex with a bunch of different women. Fights, crime, gambling, parties and of course daily drug deals. Luckily I moved out of there only a few weeks before their house was raided by cops. As a community we understand the importance of laws for creating safety in our community. In physics, scientists do their best to understand the laws that govern the universe and movement. What about with creating your dream lifestyle and success? If this universe is governed by laws wouldn't your success also be?

It also really goes to show, how much one person's life can turn around. Your life is no different. All this 'stuff' feels like a lifetime ago for me, it feels like it wasn't even real. I could never imagine in a million years doing many of the things I did all those years ago. Everyone has the potential to change, unfortunately most people just won't. They get comfortable. You have the potential to change and be whoever you wish. Understanding the laws in this chapter will set you on the right path to being that person.

We know the law of sound exists and the human ear can generally hear sounds with frequencies between 20 Hz and 20 kHz (the so-called 'audio range'). We also know that sound travels at roughly 750 miles an hour through the air but four times faster at around 3000 miles per hour in water. Everything in the universe as we know it is governed by universal laws just like these. Are we not a part of the universe? Are we not made up of energy, just like everything else in the universe?

Since we are a part of the universe and not separate to it, then we too are also governed by its laws, which are known as universal laws. There are hundreds of these laws maybe even thousands that if we researched close enough we could agree in our realm of reality are true as per the two above.

However in this book I will be unravelling the most impactful seven laws in my own personal journey that through understanding and living congruently with I have used in my favour in creating success and turning my dreams into reality. Now you can too, well if you choose to.

If you choose to live harmoniously with and understand them, embrace them and utilise them you too can use them to your advantage and find achieving success in many areas of your life much easier. Why fight these laws you cannot ultimately control, why create more resistance in your life when you can simply accept them as being natural ingredients to the simple recipe of our reality? Because when you do, not only will you find winning the inner game much easier, but winning the outer game as well. The most important factor in winning the outer game is understanding, believing and living harmoniously with these seven laws and embracing them. Understand them, utilise them to your advantage and join the small percentage of the elite that have won the inner-outer game of life with happiness, abundance and true fulfilment.

The law of causality

You see there is only one constant. One universal. It is the only real truth: causality. Action. Reaction. Cause and effect.

—The Merovingian (The Matrix)

You may have heard the saying, "for every action there is an equal and opposite reaction". The law of causality is the law of cause and effect. For every cause there is an effect.

CAUSE -> EFFECT

Out there, outside of us there seems to be much governed by laws that does not seem to comprise of consciousness (or is there?), hence the formation of the word to describe this law above: reaction. I believe the word reaction presupposes the lack of control. A tree is just a tree it cannot choose to be anything else, it cannot choose to walk up and leave. A rock is a rock and cannot make a choice, if we throw it, it's at the mercy of these laws and the chain reaction takes place. We as humans however have a window of opportunity to choose, which is why personally when talking about the law of causality in the human plane, I prefer to use the term 'response'. This gives us a sense of control and power making us the ones responsible for our own lives.

Cause and effect takes place outside of us, inside of us and also between others and other objects. When we eat unhealthy food (cause/action) the response may be one of feeling bloated, full or as some may say 'gross'. Of course choosing to eat the food in the first place is a response of our thoughts about thinking about eating the food and making the choice. Every word we speak to another will cause some kind of reaction or response. Our words will influence good feelings or bad feelings, however that is up to them to unconsciously or consciously choose and not your responsibility. It's your responsibility to understand it's not what others say to you that determine how you feel but rather your interpretation of what they say.

Has there ever been a time when someone said something that really hurt or upset you, then later when you thought about it you realised that you had overreacted? Or alternatively has there ever been a time when someone actually said something really hurtful to you but it didn't seem to faze you in the slightest? If we all walked around letting what others say about us and experiences out there determine how we feel then we would constantly be living at the mercy of others and circumstance. Wouldn't you rather feel more in control and choose your response?

You have the power and ability to make a stand right now and stand guard at the door of your mind. To choose to no longer be seduced by social conditioning or the easy way out of reacting through unconscious conditioning. When someone drives down the street and cuts you off, why give them 60 seconds of your power and happiness? Why give them more energy and focus. As Jim Rohn has said, instead of getting frustrated and giving them your power, become fascinated and wonder why they are doing it in the first place. Frustration leads to pain, fascination leads to learning. Would you rather feel pain, or would you rather learn? I understand some days can be, well, very fascinating, and that's life. But you do still have a choice, even though it may not feel like it at the time. It's simply about conditioning yourself.

Unfortunately a majority of people live at the effect side of the equation. The symptoms side. Believing things happen to them and they are not the cause and that everything else in their life is the cause. They blame the weather, the economy, the government, the media, even their own kids and family. Living at the effect side of the equation relinquishes your power and you surrender all control and responsibility, living your life at the mercy of others and circumstance. Hoping things will get better but not taking control of their own mind and their own life. The athlete of the mind and the person who is successful, fulfilled and lives their dream lifestyle lives at the cause side of the equation. They understand and believe things don't happen to them (although it definitely seems that way sometimes) but rather that things happen because of them. They are the cause of everything in their life because of the choices they make.

If you are driving down a street in a car and someone crashes into your behind, it may not be your fault, however you still play a role in that experience. It was your choice to get in and drive the car, it was your choice to drive down that particular street and those choices caused the experience to happen because without those choices it would have not happened, right? Therefore you are also responsible. I know this is a tough concept to grasp at first and you might not believe it in the beginning, although if you've come this far in this book I'm guessing you would as you are open minded. Wouldn't you agree that this belief will empower you with a sense of control and responsibility allowing you to shape your own life and destiny? Understanding this law and living congruently with it is absolutely crucial for you winning the inner-outer game of life and achieving your definition of happiness and success. Utilising your four powers in this book will also assist you in beginning to take full responsibility of everything in your life.

Some people believe everything happens for a reason, as do I. It's a belief that serves me and has helped me through the tough times. I'm sure if you asked most of the people in this book they too would share this belief. This law proves to us that everything really does happen for a reason, hence cause and effect. Seeing the seed of opportunity in every adversity we face allows us to directionalise our mind in a proactive and solution-focused way. It guides us through the tough times, the hardship and the pain to stand up and face it and understand strength grows from resistance. This day too shall pass.

Ask yourself in 12 months from now will this really matter?

What have I learned from this experience? How will this make me grow, make me stronger and make me a better person? I truly believe if I didn't face all that pain and suffering when growing up I wouldn't be driven now in helping others turn their dreams into a reality and sharing my story openly in the hopes of it inspiring people to make it through the tough times and achieve greatness in their own lives.

What is the purpose of your pain? What is the purpose of your adversity? Maybe the lessons from that painful experience are necessary to allow you to grow into the person you need to become to face future challenges and perhaps make a difference in this world. You are special, you have greatness within you. There can be no pleasure without pain. There can be no strength without resistance and there can be no learning without mistakes. I'm no better than anyone else, just simply someone who has made more mistakes than most and hopefully I have learnt from them and can share my learning with others, hoping to inspire others to get through the tough times, to face adversity, to break free from the chains of mediocrity and achieve the greatness they are destined for. It's a little corny but true. You have so much potential and when you choose to embrace the philosophies in this book as thousands have before you, you will begin to see the light at the end of the tunnel. Embrace the laws, model the successful and you too, like them can achieve greatness. Greatness comes from helping the masses. How can you help the masses? How can you add value to your community and society? How can you inspire and make a true difference in this world?

So how can you begin to make the shift from living at effect to living at cause? How can we begin to take full control and responsibility for our own lives? As in the mental vitamins in this book, it all starts with thought and our self-talk. In linguistics cause -> effect is a type of sentence, usually using bridging words like 'make', 'made' and 'because'. Start noticing when you use these words if you are referring to yourself and your four powers or something outside of you. If you are referring to something outside of you there is a good chance you are reacting and living at effect.

For example, when we say that someone makes us feel a certain way, it presupposes or suggests that we have no control over it. Many say that's what love is. People make us feel love. Who doesn't want to feel more warmth all over? Embrace the love and embrace the joy and pleasurable feelings associated with it.

Now, however, notice when you use it in a negative term. She makes me angry. We are blaming her for our anger and relinquishing control or responsibility, which means we cannot do anything about it. She makes me act in a certain way. The traffic made me late. He made me do it. These kinds of statements go hand in hand with pointing blame and is cause and effect language. Begin to switch the power dynamics to your own response-ability and change your words from other referent (another person or outside stimulus) to self-referent or yourself and start to take control then you will begin to be able to influence more effectively how you feel. You are the captain of your own life and the master of your own soul.

The law of requisite variety

The law of requisite variety states that the element within a system that has the most flexibility will also have the most influence. I guess you could say that this is the law of flexibility. I'm sure you've heard of the insanity principle before made famous by Albert Einstein: "The definition of insanity is trying to achieve a different result by doing the same thing over and over again and attempting to get a different result."

Once there was this fly and he was buzzing around the window as he could see through the glass was freedom, a beautiful sunshiny day. He flew into the glass and bounced off the glass, then kept trying harder and harder over and over butting into the glass to try to break free until he ended up dying at the windowsill and it was over. Not realising ten feet to the right was an open doorway. If only he had have effortlessly tried something different and simply veered to the right and flown out, he would be free. The fly never thought of that. Are you working harder and harder trying to get a different or better result? What have you not thought of trying or doing yet? How long will you continue to bash into the glass before you die? Or will you manoeuvre effortlessly to do something you've never done and achieve something you've never had?

Have you ever lost your keys and you start to look for them where they would normally be? You look in the kitchen, you look in the drawer, and you check your jacket, then the bathroom and run out of places to look so you go back to where you started? You've already looked there, surely they won't be there now? Well unless your partner has played a trick on you.

The level of thinking that has gotten you to where you are today is not high enough to get you to where you want to be. If you want something you don't yet have you are going to have to do something you have never yet done. Would you like more in life? More money? Start a business? Travel the world? In growing and becoming better to achieve greater results in any area we must truly understand this law.

Be flexible in your approach. If something isn't working do something differently. If you are not on the path to success, maybe it's time for a new path. Maybe it's time to ask yourself some different questions.

As human beings we have been a successful species because of our ability to evolve and adapt to our environment. What do you need to do to adapt? Not fit in, but make it work. What are you fighting? What resistance are you creating?

The law of duality

As mentioned previously in this book we live in a world of duality. Light and dark, hot and cold, up and down, pleasure and pain, in and out. What other examples can you think of? We could go on for ages. Hot could not exist without cold, light could not exist without dark, and pleasure could not exist without pain. They are measured on the same continuum or scale. If there was no pain you would not have anything to compare it to, so how would you know if something was pleasurable? The brain works with associations, connections and comparisons. This is how we learn by creating a connection between a known reference and an unknown reference. When we get confused it means we are about to learn something.

It's simply the brain creating new neural pathways by linking two reference points to make sense of something. Without confusion there can be no learning. It is the bridge between the known and the unknown, confusion and understanding in our minds.

The most powerful lessons to understanding, associated with this law, is that of the inner-outer world. To us there cannot exist one without the other. This book is built largely on this one universal law. We can spend time thinking and going into a trance and in our own minds, or we can go uptime and focus on what's outside of us using sensory acuity and being aware of our surroundings. The person or character who comes to mind having mastered this is Sherlock Holmes, or even the character Dr House modelled from Sherlock. The ability to problem solve and use lateral thinking as well as being able to simultaneously be perceptive of his surroundings.

There are a myriad of people who have mastered or won either the inner or outer game yet haven't mastered or won both. I believe the secret to true fulfilment and success is mastering and winning both worlds. I would be lying if I said I had. I like you am still on a journey of mastery. Some say mastery is a journey not a destination as I agree. I like you am someone who wants to make the most of life by creating a magical life for my loved ones and making a difference in the community and lives of others as I do. To do this we need to understand this law at the deepest level. If we spend too much time in trance and in our own heads we can neglect the people we care about most. And if we spend too much time in the outer world putting others first all the time it can be at the detriment to ourselves and our own health.

We need to find a balance between spending time focused on the inner and outer world. Sometimes there will be dark times, there will be pain, and there will be sadness. However there will also be times of joy, happiness, abundance, pleasure and freedom. Knowing when to spend which moment inside or outside of own minds takes time and eloquence and something I'm still working on. I believe this to be one of the most crucial components of winning this game we call life.

The law of flow

Energy flows where attention goes as determined by intention. Simply put, what we focus on is where our energy goes and we will experience more of, and what we focus on expands. We could also call this the law of energy. Wave-particle duality has been accepted by physicists since the days of Einstein. Wave-particle duality is a theory that proposes that every elementary particle exhibits the properties of not only particles, but also waves. I know this may be a little deep but stick with me.

You see movement is life. Right now the earth we are on is rotating at a speed of up to 2000km an hour, yet we feel stationary. Even inanimate objects like rocks that we were taught in school are solid, quantum physics now suggests that in fact, everything is made up of energy. The rock too is made up of atoms with electrons that are also moving at increasing speeds.

You might be thinking, that's great Jason but how does this help me in creating success in my life? Well our minds and our bodies are a part of the universe and are governed by this law also. Emotion comes from motion, motion comes from focus, and focus comes from intention, or in other words our why. When we know and shape our intention, it is the driving force that creates all movement and the choices we make in our life. Does that mean the end justifies the means? Not always. However it is about to become consciously aware of your intention. Being clear on your intention will also answer many of the questions as to why you do anything. Remember you can also choose your intention.

It's a common term in business and success that people say to push harder. I don't believe in pushing harder that goes against the flow. We want to utilise this flow like we would deflect an attacker. Instead of blocking him and using his force to create resistance, utilise his momentum against him and execute an effortless counter-attack. Have you been pushing harder and harder, just to find yourself facing more and more resistance? Be like water and harness the power of flow energy.

Lastly it's important to understand command negations. A command negation in NLP is known as a negative command. For example 'I will stop feeling angry', 'I wish I wasn't broke', 'I wish I had less bills'. The brain recognises the key words; angry, broke and bills. This is why what we focus on we get more of. When we think about something our actions and behaviours are in alignment with, the brain cannot lie to itself. It is a protective mechanism.

Here is an example: don't think of me in a mankini right now. Haha. Or don't think of Donald Trump in the shower, right NOW! Sorry Donald.

Did you think of it? You did right? If I say don't think of a pink elephant right now. In order for you to not think of the pink elephant you must first think of the pink elephant. Until it gets stuck in your mind, and that is now all you can think about. It's like it has permanently ingrained itself right there in front of your eyes.

In which areas of your life are you using command negations and attracting more of what you don't want into your life? Remember energy flows, where attention goes as determined by intention. This is why I'm a massive believer of the golden rule. No matter what, never say a bad thing about another person or company. All you are doing is focusing on them and giving them your power, and energy. For every minute you focus your energy on them that distracts you from your own purpose, mission or goal right now. Why give them your energy? It's not that you are better than them it's simply that you are better than that behaviour. Rise up and be a better person. Focus with positive language on what you want, and endure your intention that is good and from the heart. Always be kind and lead by example for the people you love in your life, it shows strength, fortitude, leadership and character.

The law of attraction

Have you ever bought a shirt, a dress or even a car then noticed it everywhere? Ever wondered why that is? This has been called 'schema' and several other labels in psychology and other psychological modalities. Is there the same amount of that car, dress or shirts as before? Of course, right. The difference now is you notice it. It wasn't an attractor for you before, it didn't stand out. What we look for in life we find. If we look for the good in something we will find it, if we look for the bad we will also find it.

The law of attraction has become a popular topic as of late especially since the book and documentary *The Secret* was released. It gained a lot of controversy for several reasons. Personally I really enjoy *The Secret* because although many have criticised it for not offering the 'how-to', the action after the visualisation and more information to guarantee success and attainment of your goal. What it does do is give people hope. In a world with much despair, pain and hopelessness I don't believe we can have too much hope. People criticise quotes and what appear to be band-aid fixes, and although to a degree I agree. Sometimes it's just nice to watch a silly, funny animal video, a loving video, read a warm positive quote or hear something that warms our heart. Besides isn't that what life is really about, creating warm, loving and magical moments in our life, and doing the same for others?

Just like a magnet that has a magnetic field and attracts ferrous objects like pieces of iron, steel, nickel and cobalt. Our brain and the thoughts it has creates an electro-magnetic field. This isn't science-fiction, this is now science-fact (well as much as anything can be a fact to us). In Quantum Physics they have discovered that when we think our thoughts emit energy and when our thoughts become emotionalised they become magnetised, attracting similar and like forces and thoughts. I can understand how some people would find this difficult to believe, so I invite you to do your own research and you will begin to uncover the plethora of scientific research completed in this area.

Hopefully now you can begin to understand how all these laws work together. As Stephen Hawking has spent his entire life's work attempting to find a universal theory of everything, all he has seemed to unravel at this time is a universe with a multitude of laws that work harmoniously and succinctly with each other. They all have their purpose and whether we agree with them or not or believe them or not they are at work. They can be working for us or against us and the choice is ours.

This is why visualising is a powerful tool. I have mentioned countless names and examples of success stories in this book of people who have used visualising as a means to bridge the gap from where they are now to where they want to be.

I truly believe again I would not be where I am today without this law. I spend literally hours a day in contemplation and planning internally through visualising myself in an associated form (through my own eyes) having achieved the incredible feats I dream of in my life. Thinking about them is not enough though. We must also notice the feelings and manifest and intensify those feelings as we visualise them every single day without fail until it is a reality.

Anyone that has achieved anything great that says they haven't utilised the power of this law, was doing it unconsciously. Day-dreaming is a part of being a visionary and doing extraordinary things in this life. Affirmations are also a controversial topic. There are many success stories and many disbelievers. I have personally found that for those who haven't yet formed the daily habit of visu-alising their dreams, associated and emotionalised, it is a good way to create the habit. It's not as much about creating the belief, goal or dream but more about habituating the creative visualisation process, which gives affirmations their power.

For those who have already formed the burning desire and daydream about their dreams every day, perhaps affirmations aren't necessary. However most people still living in the rat race that are not living their dream life have not yet formed this habit, so in all our coaching programs we assist people in creating the habit of daily emotionalised visualisation through using affirmations.

The challenge here is this law is constant and in flux, and con-stantly in motion, and many people are attracting more of what they don't want in their life. More pain, suffering, negative people, debts. We need to switch our focus to the positive, align our intention and create a daily habit of emotionalised daily visualisa-tion. Simply spending five minutes each day dreaming about what you want, seeing it through your own eyes, feeling the feelings it gives you and intensifying them. This could be just the instigating game changer that you need to turn your life around. Hope and faith are the seeds necessary for planting, to create your dream life and fulfilment. Start with faith. Start with hope. Start with belief!

The law of expansion

Some people call it the law of increasing returns, the law of reciprocity. It's also been known as the law of increase. What we give so too shall we receive. What we give we shall receive ten times in return and so on. Some people even call it karma. I believe the law of abundance is a part of the law of expansion. There is more than enough to go around, because just like everything is laws in flow, everything is ultimately expanding. Even the universe itself, apparently is expanding.

Even when a flower dies it leaves behind a hundred seeds to expand. Even when we leave this world we have an opportunity to pass on our knowledge and expand through having children. It's natural for us to want to expand as it's a natural law of the universe. To expand our knowledge, to expand quantitatively as well as qualitatively. Improve the quality of our relationships and the quantity of our financial abundance.

Why fight this law? When we work with these laws everything seems easier, the universe likes ease. How effortlessly does a flower grow? Without any resistance right? Have you ever found something that just seems to happen easily for you and naturally? That's because you were working in alignment with these laws, your thoughts and actions were conducive to the offspring of what this law produces.

It's only in our consciousness that we fight and create resistance with this law. We have formed limiting beliefs that say things like, 'money doesn't grow on trees' or 'it's bad to desire money', or 'you cannot be religious or spiritual and have abundance of money'. These are manmade beliefs and not the way of the universe. These limiting beliefs spawned out of scarcity frames of people you have interacted with or experiences you have had. Beliefs are not true or untrue only thinking makes them so.

I understand you might choose to not believe any of these laws. That doesn't make them untrue, we know through seeing with our own eyes the law of expansion as per the examples above. In regards to abundance, and there's more than enough to go around, ask any of the people in this book and I guarantee they too share the belief of abundance and there being more than enough to go around. Wouldn't it benefit you to release yourself from all that scarcity and negativity and truly believe in abundance and that there is more than enough to go around? Would god really create a world that didn't have enough for everyone? We have been equipped with the four powers so we can make a choice in taking control of our own life and to make a choice to embrace these laws no matter what we label them.

Start having faith and believing that there is more than enough to go around and watch the opportunities present themselves in substantial ways that weren't there before. Things that once seemed hard will become easy, and conflict that once plagued your mind will disappear for good. Expand your mind by challenging (not doubting) all your current beliefs as they are not true or untrue, do they serve you or are they holding you back from achieving the life you truly deserve and can give to others?

The law of positioning

If I was on a diet and there was chocolate in the fridge, I would eat it!
—Jason Grossman

When I make the decision to eat really healthy, I'm as disciplined as they come. However if I come home at the end of a day and I'm starving I rush to the fridge and staring back at me is an open packet of chocolate. I look over my shoulder and no one is around, I'm going to reach in and grab one of the delicious pieces of chocolaty goodness and eat It. Then do what many of us would do and eat the entire packet.

This is what I refer to as the law of positioning. If I didn't positon the chocolate in the fridge in the first place, I could not have eaten it. It's that simple. If you don't want to eat it don't buy it in the first place. If you don't want a certain experience don't position yourself in that way in the first place. Have you ever heard of a really successful person say they were in the right place at the right time? Many times, right? Just like the saying, in the wrong place at the wrong time.

When a 16-year-old boy starts learning martial arts, what does he want to go and do, fight people in the street? What is he not good at yet? That's right fighting. He positions himself in the way by focusing on it and giving himself a chance to get into that situation. Over time as he gets 10, 20 or even 30 years of experience he realises that it's not about using his skills to hurt others, but rather to help others, and what happens? He finds himself in more situations to help rather than hurt others.

Relationships are another perfect example. I believe it's gutless and totally unnecessary to strike a female or any person for that matter. The only time I would find myself in an altercation of any kind was if I thought it was a last resort to protect myself or another living being. The relationships we attract and are in, we have put ourselves there, and although it seems a little harsh we still play a part in the responsibility. When I was young my mum was beaten by her partner. She chose to be in that relationship through the law of positioning. She then also made the choice to get out of the relationship and go into hiding in a women's refuge. When I was a heroin addict living on the streets I positioned myself there and chose my relationships. I then had to dissociate from all of them as I knew it was the only way out of that life, and I also went into hiding from those people.

If you are a female and feel that you attract the wrong kind of guys, maybe you do. Maybe it's the law of positioning, it's conditioning and habitual for you. If you are reading this and you are a woman, you deserve to be treated like a lady, you deserve respect and kindness. So too do men. Well, treated kindly. Not all people are going to give us that, and sometimes finding that is easier said than done. If this is you, then doing what you've done up until now hasn't worked. So it's you, you need to change and work on you. Maybe it's time for a change, by changing yourself, loving yourself more, having a better self-image and also connecting with different people. It all starts with positioning. Positioning yourself emotionally, positioning yourself environmentally and positioning yourself with certain people and values.

In what way have you positioned yourself to minimise your

chance of success? Do you need to get out of the hood? Do you need to get out of your environment? Are there people keeping you back in your life? Are there pullers, pulling you down? Isn't it time you left them behind?

We also position ourselves with our beliefs and values. Our beliefs and values are normally our gauge for the people we attract into our life or attracted to on any level. Position your beliefs and values in a way that the super successful do and find success coming to you, rather than you to it.

What massive change do you need to make in your life right now? Maybe it's something that's so tough or so hard it almost seems like you cannot do it. That's what lets you know you must. You must move, you must stop associating with those people, you must leave your town, and you must leave that relationship. What is holding you back that is detrimental to your health, safety and future? Then how can you position yourself in a way so that you are guaranteed success?

Attend the courses, seminars, workshops, start associating with certain circles of people, go to certain locations, say yes to all opportunities and start positioning yourself for success today. What drastic change can you make today that would position yourself in a way where you are ten times more likely to achieve your dreams or goal? Now, it's time to get up and do it!

Remember persistence beats resistance. Are you resisting these natural laws? God wants you to be happy, the universe has been created in a way that allows you to live a happy and fulfilling life with abundance. But we must recognise these laws and live harmoniously with them. There are many other laws, can you think of any? However these are the ones I have most benefited from by living congruently rather than resisting. Since I have, my life has gone from a hell on earth to what some might call a fairy tale. Experiencing pain, and setback after setback. Isn't it time you left that hell behind you? Isn't it time you were truly happy? Isn't it time you lived a truly dream lifestyle with fun and fulfilment? Travel the world, help others, spend time with your loved ones, leave a legacy and create freedom and fulfilment in the lives of everyone you come into contact with.

You are special, you deserve greatness, you are the only you to ever walk this earth. Now is the time to put the past behind you. To leave that old hate and fear behind you. To take action, step up and be a man or a woman. It's time to step into your greatness and live harmoniously with these seven laws, utilising and harnessing their power along the way.

At the end of the day I'm no expert in this area by any means. I'm simply a man that was a high school dropout, spent time on the streets and has now learnt some big lessons from his mistakes along the way. I'm simply sharing with you my story and the things that have helped me personally and you can take from it what you will. Use it all, use some or use none. You are your own person, you've got to make up your own mind. If there is just one or two things you pick up from each chapter that inspire you, gives you some specific tools and help you on your journey then I'm a happy man.

True law is right reason in agreement with nature; it is of universal application, unchanging and everlasting; it summons to duty by its commands, and averts from wrongdoing by its prohibitions.

—Cicero

10

UTILISE POWERFUL LEVERAGE

The secret to leverage is to become the architect that is the innovator and creator. Then develop a formidable team of mentors, coaches, advisors and labourers that evolve into a community with a mission to transform your dream into a reality.

—Jason Grossman

It was any normal day for me at that stage of my life. I had just awoken from my afternoon nap after a workout at the gym and a morning full of personal training clients. I had a shower and got dressed putting on my bright yellow shirt that was our PT uniform and started walking to the gym where I worked just eight minutes walk from my home.

I walked into the gym saying hello to the reception staff and placed my bag and belongings in the PT office and waiting for me was the State Personal Training Manager. He looked at me almost with a scowl and said, "Jason we need to talk."

Whenever someone says your name, followed by 'we need to talk' you know it's not going to end well for you. He continued by saying that it was in the company's best interest that they relieve me of my position as a personal trainer that pays rent (contractor), effective immediately and to collect all my belongings and he was to escort me out the building and I was never to return for any reason whatsoever.

He walked me upstairs to the gym floor to collect the remainder of my belongings and waiting there was my first of ten clients that I had booked for that afternoon who had all paid $100 an hour for my services. I wasn't even allowed to speak to the client and was informed that if I attempted to contact any of my 30 clients in any way they would pursue legal action.

I was escorted out of the gym with no notice there and then with clients waiting to train with me, and here is the kicker I had been working at that gym as the busiest personal trainer in Western Australia for eight years, pretty much to the week.

I had been working hard for eight years and then just like that, I had nothing. No clients, no income and with bills to pay. That was a big learning experience for me because I vowed never to live Groundhog Day, week or year again. I had been working hard for eight years and each year was just like the year before. I did all the work as a self-employed contractor and if I didn't work I didn't get paid. This is one of the biggest reasons that people do not create financial freedom or their dream lifestyle. This was when I realised that I needed to begin to harness the awesome power of leverage.

I made a pact that from then on whenever I would work it would be to create something that would grow and work without me. Now I haven't yet explained why they let me go. I had accepted a position in management at another gym only five minutes down the road, so I do not blame them or hold a grudge, in fact quite the opposite. I can understand why they did what they did. My focus was on what I could control and after six months at the new gym they also let me go (even though I broke every Australian record in the business) and this is when I realised that I was unemployable. I could not work for anyone else in any way shape or form, not even as a contractor.

Do you work hard day and night but feel like you are living Groundhog Day? Do you exchange your time for money as a way of living? Feel like you work harder and harder just to get by and pay your mortgage or bills? The only way you can get out of this rat race of working harder, longer and more, is to create leverage. You only have 168 hours a week in your life, there's only so much you can do yourself. Isn't it time you set yourself free, free up your time, money, resources and create more freedom in your life?

I remember attending a seminar many years ago and the presenter spoke a word I had never heard: ephemeral. It has several similar meanings although the meaning he gave it was basically less is more. How to do less work and get greater results. I thought well that's a bit of an oxy-moron. He then continued speaking about the art of 'less is more'. How can we spend less time working in a job or business and create more financial abundance? How can we spend less money and get more return on our investment? How can we get more input from our output?

This simple paradox fascinated me, the thought that it is possible to put less energy and effort into something and get greater results. How is this even possible? I became an avid student of 'less is more', now an axiom to me. I began to notice that all the greatest business men and women either consciously or unconsciously had this belief ingrained deep within them. In fact many of the people alive whose stories I have read have also faced pain and adversity to turn it into massive success. They not only followed the principles of this axiom, they lived them and mastered them. Most people in this book are perfect examples of people who have mastered the art of ephemeralism and created such tremendous leverage in their lives that it is awe-inspiring. They almost make it seem easy, like they are lucky, or special.

Archimedes once said, "Give me a lever long enough and I can move the world." Levers are used in everyday life, we cannot live or perform without them. Our musculoskeletal system uses three main types of levers to perform everyday movement. We use levers in machines and equipment every day to make tasks easier and more efficient. In fact without levers we would not even exist. Leverage is what creates ease and efficiency in all aspects of this world in the context of movement.

The more efficient and stronger the levers of our body, the more power we have to move and the stronger we are. The more energy efficient we also become. The more efficient and stronger the levers are in our life, the more power we have to achieve our desired outcomes in any area of our life. Achieving our dream lifestyle is no different. Creating financial freedom is no different.

As the body uses three types of levers for maximum efficiency, we too have a number of types of levers at our disposal that we can use for achieving our dream lifestyle. In this book I have structured them into four main categories. To truly achieve our dream lifestyle we must understand and use all four types of leverage to their fullest capacity. If you want to grow or improve in any way, then that is change and change requires movement. In this world movement cannot take place without some kind of leverage. If you want to create more freedom, time, money, happiness or abundance of any kind in your life then understand and master these four forms of powerful leverage as all the other greats in this book have and you too will reap the vast rewards. You are the captain of your own ship, I'm simply the rudder here to help steer you in the right direction for smoother sailing and with greater ease, just as a lever does.

People Leverage

Let's say you are self-employed or have a job, the only way you can earn more money is by working longer and harder or increasing your prices, which are both forms of leverage. Although when used by you alone, they are not powerful forms of leverage and it puts additional stress on the fulcrum, you. The fulcrum (you) can only perform and do so much with the leverage you have. To achieve more we need to increase our leverage.

If you were to hire a second person you have now doubled your leverage, or have you? What if you bring on board a third person, is that simply triple the output and efficiency? Does it multiply? Or increase exponentially? Exponentially right, so it also has a compounding effect.

If you are on your own you are alone, if there's two of you there is a partnership, but when there are three or more you have a team and a powerful force to be reckoned with. The ultimate level of mastery is to then evolve your team into a community. A community is like a team but with much more emotional muscle, and more personal investment into the cause and the mission.

You've probably heard the saying: "many hands make light work", but what about many minds?

Here are four strong suggestions for increasing your leverage with people and a team to create your dream lifestyle. Before we do though it's important to understand we cannot and do not ever use people. We give people the opportunity to become better by being a part of our team and assisting them in not only achieving your vision but also their own. Delegation only works if the delegator works. Delegation is not enough, if it's missing the fuel for the fire. You must lead your team by living congruently to your values and living the principles you wish to teach.

Leaders become great, not because of their power, but because of their ability to empower others.

—John Maxwell

Create a mastermind

A mastermind is when a group of three or more people work harmoniously together on a project or mission and each contribute playing to their personal strengths to the completion of that mission. By forming a knighthood of the round table if you will, it will allow you to drastically increase creativity, ideas, knowledge, your network, resources and more. Walt Disney understood the power of a mastermind. Whenever Disney had a new idea for a ride, attraction or project, he would dedicate an entire wall in his office for everyone from the janitor up to the CEO in his business to contribute and add their ideas about how they could make the project even better in any way that even Disney himself might not have thought of.

Disney understood that no one is smarter than everyone together. A mastermind allows you to tap into a much deeper river of creativity and ideas to solve problems in a way you may never have thought of. It's also much easier for others to look at something from a different perceptual position. If you are in the trenches you can only see a few feet ahead of you. Someone on the outside can see exactly where you are heading and see it from a different viewpoint, giving you information and input otherwise not even conceived. Remember you cannot see the picture when you are the frame. If you are the architect of your vision and mission then your mastermind is your fellow architects for qualitative accountability.

If you have completed all the previous chapters and you are ready to really start taking action towards achieving your dream lifestyle, now is the time to create your mastermind team.

Your mastermind team can include, but is not limited to, the following:

- A business or lifestyle design coach
- Mentor
- Other business owners
- Your partner or spouse
- A business partner
- Legal and accounting advisors
- A group of peers meeting regularly for a casual catch up

In Napoleon *Hill's Think and Grow Rich* (still one of my all-time top five favourite books) he refers to a mastermind as the following:

The Mastermind principle consists of an alliance of two or more minds working in perfect harmony for the attainment of a common definitive objective.

No two minds ever come together without a third invisible force, which may be likened to a 'third mind.' When a group of individual minds are coordinated and function in harmony, the increased energy created through that alliance becomes available to every individual in the group.

Mark Zuckerberg, you know the Facebook guy right? He understood this idea. He invited five guys to his dorm room with the idea of Facebook in his mind. Only two people showed up, now all three of them are billionaires.

Have a coach or mentor

Ever heard the story of the giant ship engine that failed? The ship's owners tried one expert after another, but none of them could figure out how to fix the engine. Then they brought in an old man who had been fixing ships since he was a youngster. He carried a large bag of tools with him, and when he arrived, he immediately went to work. He inspected the engine very carefully, top to bottom.

Two of the ship's owners were there, watching this man, hoping he would know what to do. After looking things over, the old man reached into his bag and pulled out a small hammer. He gently tapped something. Instantly, the engine lurched into life. He carefully put his hammer away. The engine was fixed! A week later, the owners received a bill from the old man for ten thousand dollars.

"What?!" the owners exclaimed. "He hardly did anything!"

So they wrote the old man a note saying, "Please send us an itemised bill."

The man sent a bill that read:

Tapping with a hammer .... $ 2.00
Knowing where to tap .... $ 9,998.00

Effort is important, but knowing where to make an effort in your life makes all the difference. A coach or a mentor does exactly this. A teacher will tell you what to see but a coach or mentor will show you where to look. A teacher will give you great teachings and give you simple strategy. But a coach or mentor will also ask you the right questions that give you all the answers you seek. One of the greatest investments you will ever make is to get yourself a mentor or coach that has achieved the things in life you desire so you can not only learn from his or her successes but also his or her mistakes.

There are many coaching businesses now, we offer business coaching and lifestyle design coaching. There are many other types of coaches and companies available to you also. Maybe funds are a little tight, and all you need is a mentor, someone to take you under their wing and guide you. Who do you know or could ask to mentor or coach you? You might be surprised to discover that they actually say yes. If you don't ask, you won't get.

Build a formal team then transform it into a community

Once you have a mastermind group, a knights of the round table that meet regularly for brainstorming, ideas and how to fast track your results with leverage and ease, you really want to create a formal team. Your formal team are usually people that you pay directly or earn income from because of a resource you have offered to them.

There is a difference between a mastermind and a formal team, and yes there are times you might have your team contribute ideas and brainstorming. But this is still slightly different as it is more formal and the intention of the mastermind is singular, to focus on achieving the main mission, in this case your definition for a dream lifestyle. The mastermind focuses primarily on the big picture and ideas. Yes the team contribute to this, however the formal team are also troops, they are the ones working with you to take action and get the hard work done. The longer and harder all the formal team work, the faster you will achieve your mission. The action takers. If you are the architect and the brains behind your vision, mission and dream lifestyle then your team are the labourers you want to look after that will turn your blueprint and plan into a reality. You first create the idea in your mind. Then you create a blueprint and plan (hopefully by using the tools in this book). Then you work with your labourers and team to manifest and create the physical and end product.

Your formal team includes, but is not limited to:
- Employees
- Contractors
- Juice Plus team
- World Venture Travel Club team
- Recruitment agencies
- Marketing and sales companies

If you are currently employed this is still relevant because in order for you to create financial freedom and leverage you need to grow a team. Even if it's simply in your direct marketing business. If you are already a business owner or even the director of a company then you will already begin to find yourself understanding the importance of this section.

You might be thinking, well I cannot afford team members. Or where do I start? What if there was a way to grow your team without spending any money? I'm here to tell you it is possible. If you continue to read on I will explain.

In the early stages of any team there will be challenges and teething problems. Especially with cash flow. So how do we determine which team members to start with first? The key here is to start team members that pay for themselves. The most critical components of a new team and business is marketing and sales. If you are not generating leads or enquiries you cannot sell your product or services and you simply cannot make ends meet.

To begin with you want to ensure you are recruiting team members that specialise in or will assist specifically with hitting your marketing and lead generation targets; Key Performance Indicators (KPIs). To ensure your business and team grow regardless of circumstances in your personal life. Remember part of this book is about assisting you to create financial freedom, which means you get paid no matter what is happening in your own life. By starting with sales and a marketing team we can start them with no income in the business as we can train them and offer them a commission (a portion of the profits) until we have enough cash flow to pay them a base or even a set wage. How can you grow your sales and marketing team right now in a way that you don't have to spend any money? Once you have more profits coming through you can hire other team members that don't directly create revenue for your business.

As you grow your team, remember the focus and goal is for you to be the architect and recruit the necessary labourers to fast track the achievement of your vision and mission. With many hands and many minds it makes less work and powerful leverage.

Once you have created a team the next step is to then transcend that team into a team of leaders creating a community.

Individually we are one drop. Together, we are an ocean.

—Ryunosuke Satoro

Have an organisational structure then create a community

If your mastermind is a knights of the round table, then your formal team forms an organisational structure. What do I mean by this? Well it's simple. If you look at a company you have say a CEO at the top of the company (from a role perspective anyway). Below the CEO you might have four heads of departments or managers. It is critical that at least one of those four heads of department know the role of the CEO in case something happens to the CEO. Just like in the military, where they have an organisational structure. If a colonel dies in war, or is discharged, there is another team member (major) that can take their place. If a major dies in war or is discharged, then there is another team member that can move up the ranks if necessary, such as a captain. Giving team members an opportunity to grow keeps them motivated and inspired, along with your mission and vision. Money does not create long-term motivation in a team – personal growth and opportunity does.

It's the same with your team. You want to ensure that you have a Second in Charge (2IC) that can take your place if necessary when you are away, and everyone is working on their level, and there is always someone who is aware of the next level above. Do you have a 2IC yet? This philosophy will ensure the continuation of your vison and mission in your business of creating your dream lifestyle. By having a strong organisational structure no matter what size or type of team you have, it will ensure the mission is still in action even if you are personally AWOL.

It's also important to understand that once you have this structure that your number one client becomes your 2IC (your frontline of the structure). Their number one clients are their frontline and so forth. This creates a chain of command, clarity and huge leverage within the team.

The organisational structure looks something like this:

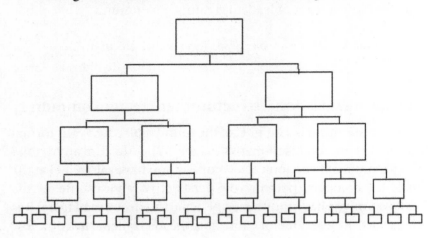

Once you have implemented all these previous steps the ultimate evolution of a team is to transcend it into a community. A community is more than a team, it's a collection of teams and sub-communities. It's a group of people that interact with one another and focus on the common goal and mission, however, the main difference is that they are personally invested in the mission as they are emotionally invested in it. They are passionate about the mission and team leaders in the community feel it is their destiny or purpose in life. When you find team leaders that are this emotionally invested in the mission you will begin to notice your team evolves from a team to a community. A place where there is complete openness for ideas and everyone contributes to the mission with ideas, concepts and ways to improve the quality and quantity of the community fast tracking the mission.

Never believe that a few caring people can't change the world. For, indeed, that's all who ever have.

—Margaret Mead

Outsourcing

If you are the team leader, the mastermind is the brain, innovation and creativity, the team are the action takers and troops. Then what about all the menial tasks that no one is really motivated to do or enjoys doing?

You know the tasks: phone calls, data entries, emails, tracking, mundane social media tasks, replying to messages. Why waste your time doing these, or having your mastermind or action takers do these, when you can pay a few dollars an hour to have someone else do them. You can also have them do graphic design, web design, SEO, social media marketing and growth, the list goes on.

Instead of wasting countless hours on all of these menial tasks have someone else do them, and delegate them to someone who actually does this specifically for a job.

The company we use is called Ezy VA (there are literally hundreds of these companies now) and for just $7-9 an hour you can have an outsourcing team take care of everything for you in the Philippines:

- Telemarketer
- Graphic design
- Web developer
- Social media
- Virtual assistant
- SEO and IT
- Website design

At least start with a Virtual Assistant for ten hours a week and free up your time for the more important stuff.

You can find out more or get yourself a virtual assistant by visiting our website: www.streetstoamillionaire.com

Wouldn't you rather spend quality time with your loved ones than doing these tasks? Then what are you waiting for?

Leaders don't wish to be managed, nor do they wish to be led. Leaders wish to have the opportunity to lead.

—Jason Grossman

Time Leverage

The following story is one told by Dr Stephen R. Covey to illustrate the importance of prioritising the different areas of our lives.

One day this expert was speaking to a group of business students and to drive home a point, used an illustration I'm sure those students will never forget. After I share it with you, you'll never forget it either.

As this man stood in front of the group of high-powered over-achievers he said, "Okay, time for a quiz." Then he pulled out a one-gallon, wide-mouthed Mason jar and set it on a table in front of him. Then he produced about a dozen fist-sized rocks and carefully placed them, one at a time, into the jar.

When the jar was filled to the top and no more rocks would fit inside, he asked, "Is this jar full?" Everyone in the class said, "Yes." Then he said, "Really?" He reached under the table and pulled out a bucket of gravel. Then he dumped some gravel in and shook the jar causing pieces of gravel to work themselves down into the spaces between the big rocks.

Then he smiled and asked the group once more, "Is the jar full?" By this time the class was onto him. "Probably not," one of them answered. "Good!" he replied. And he reached under the table and brought out a bucket of sand. He started dumping the sand in and it went into all the spaces left between the rocks and the gravel. Once more he asked the question, "Is this jar full?"

"No!" the class shouted. Once again he said, "Good!" Then he grabbed a pitcher of water and began to pour it in until the jar was filled to the brim. Then he looked up at the class and asked, "What is the point of this illustration?"

One eager beaver raised his hand and said, "The point is, no matter how full your schedule is, if you try really hard, you can always fit some more things into it!"

"No," the speaker replied, "that's not the point. The truth this illustration teaches us is: If you don't put the big rocks in first, you'll never get them in at all."

How would you like to ephemeralise your time? Spend more time on the things you love, and less on the things you don't? Would you like to quit your job? Is there something you do regularly that you despise? I personally don't like gardening or cleaning, so it's really simple that I position myself in a way so that I don't have to perform these activities. What activities would you stop doing if you could? In this section I'm going to show you how you can stop doing all those things that you despise and focus on what's really important, creating magical memories with your loved ones and giving back to the community.

It's as basic as following a simple six-step process.

Step 1 Assimilate

Step 2 Eliminate

Step 3 Automate

Step 4 Delegate

Step 5 Prioritise

Step 6 Action

By following this simple six step process you can eliminate to do lists forever. Do you ever create massive to do lists just to create more pressure and stress and not complete them?

Stop using the 'to do' list. And start truly living, by following this six step process today.

Step 1: Assimilate all the action items required completing for the day (this is not your to-do list, stay with me). Unload a list of everything and anything that needs to be completed so you feel clear and certain it is a successful day. Again this is not your to-do list.

Step 2: Eliminate anything from the list that does not really need to be on there in the first place, or does not really need to be actioned today.

Step 3: Automate. Ask yourself which action items can be automated so you never have to have them on the list again. An example might be invoicing or payments that can be made direct debit.

Step 4: Delegate. Ask yourself which action items on that list, if you are honest with yourself, you could have someone else do. Yes you are right, people might not do things exactly the same way you do, but I'm sure you will agree that they will be done sufficiently. This step normally removes most of your items for the day. Scheduling, emails, social media, phones calls can all be delegated. Graphic design, blogging, websites it can all be delegated using your out-sourcing team.

Step 5: Prioritise. By now you should only be left with around three action items. Hardly a list. Ask yourself if you were to complete just one item today to feel successful and have grown which is the most important? Then the second and third. This will be your focus for the day. This is putting your big rocks first. It can include personal action items as well as business. If you have more than three action items on the list then you have not gone through and processed efficiently enough. Go back again and I guarantee your list will shrink to a few items and no longer will it be a list.

Step 6: Action the three items on your list in order of priority, number one first and so on.

If you choose to use this simple six-step process your days will feel much less overwhelming, you will be more productive and you will enjoy them more also as you will be doing more of the things you love and less of the things you despise.

Using this strategy means you no longer need discipline as you won't need motivation to do the things you love, you already love them. You will stop procrastinating and putting things off. Increase your productivity and make more time for your family and the things you truly value.

Now is a good time to get rid of being a perfectionist as well. Instead of begin a perfectionist be a progressionist and focus on growth and constant never ending improvement each and every single day.

Here are my top ten tips for leveraging your time
1. Big rocks first (what are the three most important action items?)
2. Shorten appointments and meeting times
3. Do group appointments and meetings instead of one on one
4. Ditch your phone (I personally don't even own a phone, why do I need one?)
5. Ditch your email (I don't personally use an email, I have one set up for my VA)
6. Ditch your schedule (ban yourself from your schedule and have your VA take care of it)
7. Cluster tasks (focus your time and energy collectively on one thing or set of things)
8. Use the six-step process in this chapter
9. Structure your week and plan the length of time and when you will complete items
10. Spend time on items that will create more leverage

We each only have 168 hours in a week. Sometimes it's necessary to go to bed a little later, to get up a little earlier and leverage our own personal time. How important are your dreams to you? What are you prepared to do to achieve them? Some people say things like, "I don't have the time". Really? We all have 168 hours a week. It's what we choose to do with that time. It's what is most important to us and what we value most. What we value most is where most of our time goes. Start controlling your week and what you do with your time by choice rather than by doing what 95% of people do and react to what their life and business throws at them. Anticipate, schedule and plan then focus on productivity through the basic lessons I too have learned in this book.

Most importantly do what you love, no matter how trivial don't just try to unload everything so you aren't busy. If you enjoy it then do it, if you love doing it then keep doing it? The goal is to spend your entire days doing exactly what you love, and that is different for everyone.

Don't set business goals and then try to fit your life around those goals. Set lifestyle goals and create a business that supports that lifestyle.

—Unknown

Money leverage

As we've already spent some time in this book on financial freedom, let's use this section to streamline the basics. It's really simple, if you want to create financial freedom in your life, you need to create financial leverage. Here are what I believe to be the five most powerful ways to leverage your money in addition to the philosophy in the financial freedom chapter:

Create passive and residual income streams

Create passive and residual income streams you can forecast and budget for. Most people create a living by exchanging their time for money and minimal wage. The amount we are paid per hour or year is a direct reflection of the value we add to the market place. If we wish to earn more we need to add more value. By increasing your skills and improving your talents you can earn more per hour, however you are limited by the amount of hours in the day or week.

When we add additional income streams to our economic status it allows us to diversify and create leverage. When they are residual or passive then they are even more leveraged. There are several viewpoints on the definition and difference between residual income and passive. My personal take is simple. Residual income is income you receive by doing some work like writing a book, then you receive royalties or commission for the rest of your life, well if it sells. Hopefully this book will sell and then that gives you residual income. Typically it is a little harder to forecast and predict the income in the future as it's dependant on sales, even if you set targets there is no 100% guarantee you will exactly hit those targets.

Passive income is generally income you do literally no work for. For example you have a designer create a website and monetise the website for you on autopilot. You haven't really done anything. Another example is if you have a business and a manager hires a new staff member and that staff member creates revenue for the business that too is passive. There are many investments that will also offer great yields.

At the end of the day what is really important here is that you are creating income streams that continue to grow no matter what is happening in your personal life. You still get paid. You could go bankrupt, you could divorce your partner and they take 50%, a loved one could die, there could be illness or you might even lose a business. Regardless of whether these things take place or not, you will still get paid.

This is why I'm such a huge fan of direct marketing. It's an incredibly leveraged hedging strategy for your long-term financial success.

All it takes to take the first step to financial freedom is to create enough residual or passive income to cover your basic living expenses. For most people this is under $1000 a week. You could be doing that in the next six months, if you choose to apply the philosophies in this book. Isn't it time you stopped exchanging your time for money? Isn't it time you started living the life you truly deserve? Yes there will be doubts and fear. I'm not suggesting you quit your job. Keep your job or business and work on your living full-time. Then start working on your fortune and financial freedom part-time. Once the income from your other streams replaces your full-time job, career or business that's when you can choose to quit and exit the rat race. Imagine if you never had to work to pay your bills ever again. It's possible, if you act now.

Use compounding
As per the financial freedom chapter of this book, start learning about compounding. Start saving weekly and understand how compounding interest works. Let's be honest this one strategy alone might not set you free, but long-term over time it is a very powerful strategy for hedging your financial success.

Get used to having large sums of money in your accounts, it conditions you for wealth. Seeing those big amounts. I believe a big part of the reason why many people 'freak out' as they become more affluent is because their expenses also increase. I remember the first week into one of my businesses I had over $20,000 for that week in expenses and bills. I was like wow and to be honest I did do a little 'freak out'. My focus should have been on the fact that that week was a record revenue week for the business, however the poor mindset, or mentality, keeps us locked into small amounts. Having the opportunity to do business coaching with clients for many years now, I see this almost with every single client. Once their expenses hit a certain point they 'freak out'. If you have a business turning over $10,000,000 a year, do you think your expenses are going to be in the millions for the year? Good chance, depending on the model right? Yes keep your expenses down, but also understand we want to think like the affluent. Instead of looking at all things as an expense start asking the question: which things are actually investments? Investing in a coach for example can assist in increasing your business by up to 1000% in just 12 months. What a huge return on investment (ROI).

Let's be honest, saving and compounding alone may not create the financial freedom you desire, it is however an incredibly important part of the jigsaw puzzle. Its slight nuances, and consistently doing all the little things that create the vision and bigger picture you have for creating wealth.

If you struggle to save up until now, create an automated direct debit system each week with your bank so you don't have to even think about saving, it's simply automatic. If you really want to condition yourself and find it hard, perhaps even ask your partner or family member to have an account in their name until you create the habit of regular saving and spending less than you earn.

Use your money to make more money instead of buying stuff

What do you spend your money on? Do you buy a lot of unnecessary clothes, music, junk food, medication, cigarettes, and alcohol? Do you like to have toys? Stereos, gadgets? Phones? TVs? What about big toys? Like cars and boats?

The affluent think of money a little differently than people with a poor mindset. People look at money as a means to get things and stuff, perhaps even survive. This really is the scarcity mindset holding people back from creating financial freedom. The affluent think of money as a tool, a way to increase leverage in their life. Yes of course you can get things with it but that's not the primary focus. Poor mindset people buy a lot of unnecessary things and use all their money every week to buy clothes, food, partying, music, games and things that help them just get by. Middle-class mindset people who usually do make good money, seem to spend a lot more on bigger stuff like boats, cars, sound systems, the latest toys and gadgets.

I'm not saying to not treat yourself to a new toy. The problem here is that many people borrow money to purchase these bigger toys and accumulate more debt. They look wealthy on the surface but underneath all the toys, gadgets and mortgage they are barely keeping their head above water. Do you know anyone like this? Perhaps even intimately?

The affluent however ask themselves how can they use their money to create more money which in turn creates more leverage and freedom. How can I invest the small amount I have and exponentially grow it? You will need to become more frugal. You will need to spend more wisely. You will need to become more disciplined. This is where remembering your why will keep you focused and diligent.

Next time you go to buy something ask yourself will this take me one step closer to my dream of financial freedom or two steps backwards?

Increase your borrowing capacity

Many of the wealthiest people alive are also in the most amount of debt. They understand however there is a difference between good debt and bad debt. An asset and a liability. They understand that the higher their borrowing capacity the less of their own money they need to use when a good business or investment opportunity presents itself. Plus the more money they will have at their disposal to create greater returns.

The higher your borrowing capacity the more you can borrow for an investment property or perhaps even for your own home, which will give you a larger increase in equity post-handover and not to mention a nicer place for you or your tenants to live. The higher your borrowing capacity the more you can invest, the more income you will create and the faster you will grow your net worth.

The three quickest ways to increase your borrowing capacity so you can use someone else's money is:

1. If you own a business do the right thing, the legal thing and claim all your income. The higher your net income the higher your borrowing capacity.
2. Increase your cash flow in your business or if you have a job through the direct marketing opportunities in this book.
3. Increase your net worth. Every time you increase your net worth you are also increasing your borrowing capacity. This is a big part of the reason the rich get richer. They understand and use these powerful financial leveraging strategies.

Start asking yourself today: what can I do to increase my chances of buying my first home, my first investment property, or even that investment business I've always wanted? Cash flow can set us free and net worth hedges our affluent financial status.

Some time ago I was offered a once in a life time opportunity to invest in a property that needed to be sold fast. I was the tenant at the time and the property was valued at $350,000. They offered it to me for $240K. This property was less than three years old in a rapidly growing, new community and was predicted to double in worth in the next few years.

Without blinking an eye lid I said I'm in. I organised every-thing I needed, approached the bank and after all was organised I fell short by $20,000K. Just $20K. I searched high and low to find it and could not. I asked the bank why I could not borrow that extra $20K. They informed me that it was because of the $8000 debt on my current credit card. If I had no debt on that credit card, I would have had more than enough.

I missed that opportunity because of my bad debt. That house sold less than two years later to another buyer for almost $450K. When I found out that I had missed out on over $200K because of a credit card I cut up my credit card and vowed to never use it again. If you are already well off financially and very disciplined with paying off your credit card then great. Unfortunately 80% of people (or more) are not. Think about it, why have access to a resource that makes you take steps backwards and move away from financial freedom by seducing you into buying things you don't really need, with money you don't really have?

If you are not yet financially free, I strongly recommend pulling out your credit card right now, and cut it up. Then organise a payment plan with the bank. If you need to order something online or over the phone, the solution is simple. You can use a debit card. All the benefits of a credit card without all the setbacks. How badly do you want financial freedom? Ask yourself do you really need the credit card? Is the credit card currently helping you move closer to your dream lifestyle or further away? If further away, cut it up right now and do yourself a favour and replace it with a debit card.

Borrow money when you can, not when you need
We often hear talk of the trillions of dollars of debt this world is in. My question is to who? In a world that moves so fast with such rapid changes and everything becoming easier to access, it's no surprise that people are getting into more and more debt. When we want that car, that home, that stereo, that jet ski, we go and get it, even if we don't yet have the money for it.

We spend more than we earn getting ourselves into more and more debt, until we get to a point of what seems like no return. Living within your means, increasing your cash flow then increasing your means is a habit shared by many of the financially free.

We purchase things on our credit card, push the limits on what we can currently cover for our mortgage, and are seduced by all these no interest, get now, and buy later offers. It's really simple. If you don't have the money for it right now, and borrowing the money for it won't increase your net worth or take you closer to financial freedom, it really should be a no brainer. Don't buy it. Well only if you are serious about creating financial freedom, and creating a dream lifestyle for you and your family.

We then get to a point that in order for us to just pay our bills or get by we need to get a loan or borrow money. Have you ever gotten into so much debt, you had to borrow money to get out of debt in any way shape or form? Do you really believe that kind of a habit and choice (and it is a habit and choice) is going to create the life that you dream of?

I would love to see you shaping your habits from getting into bad debt and borrowing money when you need it, to getting into good debt and borrowing money when you can. The wealthy are often borrowing money simply because they can. They are borrowing money when they can to invest in property, business and other opportunities. Think about it. You can use someone else's money that's not even yours that you didn't have to make, and then you can take that money and use it to make even more money. Umm some would call that free money.

People blame things outside of their control for the rich getting richer and the poor getting poorer but being rich or being poor is a choice. This one strategy, idea and habit is quite possibly the most powerful out of all the affluent. You might say to yourself, well no Jason it's not a choice. However it is and the only way you are going to be able to climb out of the hole or rat race you are in is to take full responsibility and make a choice to be rich. To take full responsibility for creating your current situation, because only then will it empower you with the ability to change it. It was my choice to live on the streets when I was younger. It was my choice to put the needle in my arm to shoot up heroin and it was my choice to create financial freedom by turning my life around. Make the choice now to be financially free, create the necessary habits and take the necessary action. You can do this, you are capable and yes you really do deserve it.

Next time you go to borrow money in any way ask yourself, am I using this money to take a step closer to financial freedom or a step backwards?

Banks, business angels, venture capitalists and other business owners are constantly looking for good opportunities to invest in, do you have one for them?

Improve your financial literacy and track everything

If you want to become great at something it takes practice and learning. If we want to pursue a career we need to study. We need to do it. We need the intellectual knowledge as well as the experiential knowledge. This is true to learn to drive a car, learn to fly a plane, or anything else that is outside of our basic nature, instincts and talents.

Business and finance are no different, if you want to excel you need to increase your knowledge and evolve your habits. First step as we covered earlier is to get yourself a mentor or a coach. Someone that has already achieved that which you wish to achieve to make your journey easier. Reading the books, attending the courses and seminars and also listening to the audios by people on the subject of wealth creation, business and finance is critical. I'm not saying you need to study to become an accountant, why would you do that when you can simply hire an accountant? As many super successful business owners will tell you the most important ability in business is the ability to read reports, especially financial reports. Cash flow projections will allow you to see your forecasted income each week or month.

A budget will allow you to see you forecasted expenses in the future weekly or monthly. Then a profit and loss statement will show you the actual report of how well you stuck to your budget and how consistent your income projections were. A balance sheet with a list of assets versus liabilities is also important. However in the beginning you want to condition yourself to create the reports, use the reports and learn how to use them each and every day or at least weekly.

This way when things don't go to plan, and they won't, you can make the necessary changes and improvements by pinpointing exactly where the problem lies. It takes the guess work out of it. You can then begin to read patterns and anticipate problems before they even occur.

How we feel about our finances or business is never an accurate reflection of what's actually happening in our business or financial status. I can recall a time of being asked how business was and I replied with it's amazing thanks. We have great clients, team and systems and are really happy. I then looked at our financial status and we actually ran at a loss that week. I can recall another time of being asked the same question and replying with it's not going that well actually. Then when I looked I noticed that it was the most profitable week the business had ever had.

By tracking the financial logistics of what's happening in our life and/or business it creates a dichotomy. A split between how we feel and what's actually happening in our business. It allows us to remove emotions and look at it logically to enable us to focus on solutions and keep us accountable for hitting our targets and KPIs.

Get yourself a bookkeeper, accountant, mentor and whoever else you need to point you in the right direction to start tracking your finances today and keep yourself accountable to the massive goals you have. Remember with your goals the problem isn't that we set goals too high and don't achieve them, the problem is that when we set goals too low and we do achieve them. Aim higher, think larger, track everything and work with the right people to keep you on track.

If you would like some examples or resources simply visit our website: www.streetstoamillionaire.com

Resources leverage

Henry Ford had a vision of mass marketing automobiles for the masses and he was one of the wealthiest men of his time, and most resourceful. He fully understood the importance of leveraging resources and staying at the cutting edge of technology. He went on to not only be the first to use the assembly line but also created the first V8 engine. Some men today would be very grateful.

What resources do you have at your disposal? We have more resources in today's world than ever before in history. To understand and leverage from the resources at our disposal could arguably be one of the most important factors to winning the outer game of business. There are a ton of products and services out there that you can invest in to give you access to more resources and create powerful leverage in your business, finances and even life.

- Coaching
- Technology
- Information
- Sales and marketing
- Equipment
- And much more

I believe the most important part here is what I refer to as the law of positioning as discussed in the chapter seven Universal Laws. Positioning yourself in a way you have to succeed. You must succeed, there is no other option. A coach is a perfect example of this. He or she will keep you accountable to sticking to your plan, taking the action, feeling the fear and acting anyway.

Who or what is keeping you accountable? Utilise all four of these types of leverage. Especially people and money in the beginning. And watch as your life seems to magically shift overnight with how fast the momentum builds for you in achieving your dream lifestyle.

Mark Zuckerberg wanted to create an online community. The largest in the world and he did so through leveraging the World Wide Web. Steven Jobs, Bill Gates, and many of the other tech billionaires became so successful because of the way they massively leveraged their resources. What are you not thinking of yet? What resources could you leverage from if you really wanted to?

Once you have your plan the next step is to execute your plan. Once you begin to execute your plan it's important to track your progress and refine it. By understanding and utilizing all four of these types of leverage you can really ephemeralise your finances, business, health and other areas of your life. Leverage your time, leverage through giving people opportunities to lead. Leverage through changing your beliefs about money and making the most of all the resources this incredible world has to offer. Write down one Idea you have for creating massive leverage in each of these four areas right now. Stop what you are doing, write them down, then execute them right now. Who do you have to email or call? What plan or strategy do you need to implement? Take the time to do it now. Eliminate the feeling of being overwhelmed, stressed and anxious and create massive leverage today.

Give me a lever long enough and a fulcrim on which to place it and I shall move the world – Archimedes AD 340

11

TAKE MASSIVE ACTION UNTIL!

The path to success is to take massive, determined action.

—Tony Robbins

It was one of the happiest times of my life. It was the week of Christmas and just several months beforehand the woman I was madly and deeply in love with at that time had moved in to live with me. For the first time in my life I knew what it was like to be in love. I was in my mid 20s and everything seemed to be perfect. At the time money was great, I was in great shape and I was a fool in love. We decided to have a Christmas party and entertain guests, which as you can imagine in Australia was a fairly big celebration. We had a spa, bar, games, cocktails, BBQ, music and much more set up. It was a big night. When we awoke the next morning we didn't have time to clean as we had a nearly four-hour drive ahead of us to go camping with my family.

We spent a week together with the family camping in tents. Throughout that time more and more tension for the first time ever had built between us. We had never even had a disagreement and now we could barely sit together for five minutes. When we arrived back at the house a week later, the house was a mess. I had it in my mind we would clean immediately, but she wanted to go see her dad as she hadn't seen him for Christmas yet.

We ended up in an argument both adamant about what we were going to do. We were tired and not thinking straight. She made it clear she was going to her dad's no matter what, and I turned around and said, "if you walk out that door, don't ever come back!" It was one of the biggest mistakes I had ever made. I didn't take action, in fact I did nothing, I let her walk out the door and out of my life. Several days went by before I even attempted to contact her.

We tried to make it work after that but it just seemed like The Beatles song was wrong. Love is not all you need. Due to my inaction and being a man it took me seven years to get over the pain from that relationship, which shaped the destiny of my future relationships and caused me to self-sabotage them. Failing to take action in the most critical times of your life could be the difference between years of pain and years of pleasure. Years of sorrow and years of joy. Years of sadness and years of happiness. Don't think, just act. Inaction is one of the biggest causes of regret.

It really seemed that the stars were aligned for me because within less than 12 months of finally gaining closure from that previous relationship it allowed me to meet and fall in love with the woman I am meant to spend the rest of my life with. Kailey. My rock, my girl, my world!

If you have followed this book entirely and taken the time to implement all the strategies and principles, then by now I'm sure you have begun to notice a massive shift, in the direction towards your personal journey and dream lifestyle. If you simply read this book and think to yourself, 'yes great book', you will not reap the massive rewards from the philosophies within it. Additionally, reading and acting upon this book alone will not guarantee your success. What will guarantee your success is constant never ending improvement and daily application of the principles within this book. Did you just read the book? Or did you apply and complete all the exercises? If you did simply just read it, maybe now is a good time to complete this chapter, then go back to chapter one and simply spend some time completing all the exercises. Even a week on each chapter's exercises will be very effective.

Want to know what I do every day in the shower? Well there are a few things, however I have a few rituals. I do my attitude of gratitude as in the four keys to true fulfilment; I do my visualising for the day. I also ask myself what I can do today to improve my wealth, health, relationships, spirituality and mindset. I have found creating rituals to be one of the most critical components to living a dream lifestyle. Not just a habit, a ritual is a habit backed by a burning desire with specific intention and magnificent obsession of that intention. That habit (ritual) is powered by an indelible will to succeed, because you must make that dream a reality.

Have you ever heard of or seen someone become a success overnight (besides a lotto winner)? If you have you can bet we simply haven't seen the thousands of hours behind the scenes. It takes time, years to cultivate and create a dream lifestyle. One where you simply have to pinch yourself to determine and ensure that it's real. Yes, this is me, I am awake and what an amazing life. What rituals do you need to create every single day to instil a burning desire and magnificent obsession for living your true dream life? What can you do to magnify and intensify your why? To motivate you and inspire you every day to jump out of bed as though it is on fire? To take massive action every day, build the unstoppable momentum and create your dream lifestyle?

You want to know your why, and never forget it. Know your what, (your target) and never change it, no matter what obstacles you are faced with. Plan your how and be flexible in applying it. In NLP there is a presupposition known as the Law of Requisite Variety. It simply states that the element within a system that has the most flexibility will have the most power and influence within that system.

This is why we use the process PT IT! This is the process as a personal trainer that I used for years to help thousands of people get into shape and lose weight. Know exactly where you are now and exactly where you want to be and by when. Backtrack from there to set smaller goals (micro and macro cycles) along the way. Create a specific step by step plan to achieve it (if you need experts to help then form your team). Align your psychology for success and fuel your why. Monitor every day, everything that you are doing. When things are not going to plan as you can see in your tracking, you can make the necessary changes (Law of Requisite Variety). Then continue until you achieve your goal.

As powerful a process as this is, I want to remind you of something that is critical for your happiness. Goal setting is important and so is achieving your dream lifestyle. What is even more important is to remember that life is a journey. If we spend all our time thinking about the next goal we are never truly happy. We must learn from the past, plan for the future but live in the now. Now is the only power you have to act, to speak, to feel. To experience a dream lifestyle is to understand that it is not just a destination, it is also a journey. Have your ambitious goals, set the sail to achieve your definition of a dream lifestyle, and also remember to enjoy the journey. Because when you achieve your definition of a dream lifestyle, your new definition will probably change, and do you really want to chase that goal until you die?

Set bigger goals, aim higher, step it up and play a bigger game, raise your standards and live to your full potential. Just remember to stop and smell the roses and enjoy your hard work. Remember to celebrate and reward yourself for how far you have come, the hard work you have put in and reap the rewards by sharing them with your loved ones – the whole reason you are doing it in the first place.

Now you are ready to go out into the world and make an impact, to tell the world what you are going to do but first show it. Become an 'until' person and do whatever it takes to achieve your dreams until you are successful. To become an athlete of the mind take your mental vitamins every day. Eliminate the words 'try', 'like', 'should' and 'but' from your vocabulary to eliminate all excuses and blame. To live the four keys to true fulfilment by being aware of your plan and what you need to do, manifesting and intensifying your why. To grow and become better every day, contribute and make a difference in the community. To stick to your financial freedom plan and create true abundance in all areas of your life: wealth, health, relationships, mindset and spirituality.

Follow your dreams and travel the world, live your bucket list and vision board. Then leverage the power you have to not only create an amazing life for yourself but for others as well. Because that's what life is truly about, giving. Contribution, making a difference. One day when you leave this world, all that will really matter is the hearts you touched, the lives you changed, and whether you left this world a better place by being here.

Have you ever left anything too late? Didn't have the opportunity to tell someone how you felt? Didn't follow through on a promise? The key to taking action right now is to fuel your why and apply all the techniques in this book. Reading is not enough you must apply.

When I think of leaving things too late it reminds me of an older 80s song; The Living Years by Mike and the Mechanics. Do you know it? If you do read the words below and as you do sing it in your head, and tell me it doesn't motivate you. If you don't know the song jump onto YouTube right now and read the words as you listen to it. It's a story about a young man who left it too late to tell his dad how much he loved him. Do you have pain and resentment for anyone in your family? Isn't it time you forgive them and move on? Why carry that burden? One day they will be gone, and it will be too late. If you had just 24 hours to live, who is the first person you would call? What would you say? And what are you waiting for?

'The Living Years'

Every generation
Blames the one before
And all of their frustrations
Come beating on your door

I know that I'm a prisoner
To all my Father held so dear
I know that I'm a hostage
To all his hopes and fears
I just wish I could have told him in the living years

Crumpled bits of paper
Filled with imperfect thought
Stilted conversations
I'm afraid that's all we've got

You say you just don't see it
He says it's perfect sense
You just can't get agreement
In this present tense
We all talk a different language
Talking in defense

Say it loud, say it clear
You can listen as well as you hear
It's too late when we die
To admit we don't see eye to eye

So we open up a quarrel
Between the present and the past
We only sacrifice the future
It's the bitterness that lasts

So don't yield to the fortunes
You sometimes see as fate
It may have a new perspective
On a different date
And if you don't give up, and don't give in
You may just be O.K.
Say it loud, say it clear
You can listen as well as you hear
It's too late when we die
To admit we don't see eye to eye

I wasn't there that morning
When my Father passed away
I didn't get to tell him
All the things I had to say

I think I caught his spirit
Later that same year
I'm sure I heard his echo
In my baby's new born tears
I just wish I could have told him in the living years

Say it loud, say it clear
You can listen as well as you hear
It's too late when we die
To admit we don't see eye to eye

Forgive people for you. Forget about making your parents proud, or getting approval or waiting for others to apologise or forgive you. Focus on what you can control and forgive yourself. Do this for you because you deserve it. But you must put that old story behind you. You must break free from those chains. Forgive yourself now and move on.

Work hard but play harder. Remember to celebrate, be eccentric, and be a little lavish. Make the most of special occasions, but also remember to make the most of every day. Have fun, be a little silly, be a little crazy. When you have success and kick a goal, do something to formally celebrate. Reward your team, have social events, have prizes, have giveaways. Create the element of surprise for the people that are important to you in life. Giving the gift of love through surprise is one of the most amazing feelings there are. Just remember to give yourself the gift of celebration as well. You don't want to burnout, so remember to reward yourself and not take yourself too serious. Live and laugh every day, look on the brighter side of everything.

I have just organised an annual catch up for the team which goes for three days. These three days include a day at Dreamworld theme park, jet skiing, go-karts, theme restaurant dinner and show. I surprised the team by picking them up in three real life fire engines, they had no idea. We had lunch and even had t-shirts that said 'keep calm and create your dream life'. Corny, yes. But also very fun. What can you do to create more fun in your daily environment and reward and celebrate with people you care about? Isn't it time you took your kids to Disneyland?

You can read clever motivational sayings all day, but that won't replace you getting off your butt and doing the HARD WORK!
—Darren Hardy

Recently I had the pleasure and honour of visiting Australia Zoo, the creation of Australia's own crocodile hunter the late great Steve Irwin. Steve Irwin was an incredibly passionate and genuine man that lived life to the fullest. When we visited the zoo we had an opportunity to appreciate the size of the legacy he has left. It is awe inspiring. If you are ever in Queensland, Australia be sure to add it to your bucket list. Here is a little more about his inspiring story and the incredible journey that lead to his legacy

I believe it is our responsibility once we are financially free to ensure that we leave a legacy for our children, family and the world to continue having a positive impact in creating a better world after we are gone. What are you doing to leave a legacy? How will your family be proud of you? When I do leave this world I don't want people to be sad and mourn I want them to celebrate my life and give them gifts of happiness and fulfilment as long as they are alive. Don't you?

So what do you dream of? What if I told you your dreams are possible? What if you really believed it in your heart of hearts? As you know, when I was a teenager I dropped out of high school then was kicked out of home. I lived on the streets as a heroin addict with nothing but the clothes of my back. Now I travel the world, am financially free and help thousands of people in transforming their dreams into reality. I'm no better than anyone else, if I can do it, so can you.

Your dreams are possible no matter what adversity you have faced, no matter where you are in life right now you can achieve anything your mind can conceive. I challenge you to rise up and stand up now. Transform your dreams into reality, do it for your family, do it for your loved ones, do it for your community but most importantly do it for yourself.

Take action, massive action, each and every day and never give up, never quit on your hopes and your dreams. Life is an adventure, a journey to be cherished, a smorgasbord of magical memories awaits you, but you must decide right now that you will do whatever it takes.

Yes life will knock you down, it will beat you to your knees, but you have a choice, you can stay down or you can get back up and fight and keep moving forward and keep moving towards your dreams.

Cultivate your why, manifest your why and intensify your why until you form a magnificent obsession until you cannot sleep at night because you are too excited to go to sleep, and as soon as you open your eyes in the morning you cannot wait to burst out of bed so you can continue on your adventure that could possibly be your last day on this earth.

Knowing your why means you will never quit on your dreams, never quit on your goals no matter how tough it gets, no matter how much pain you feel you remember that pain is temporary but failure lasts forever. We all feel pain don't we? We can let it shackle us in the constraints of apathy or we can embrace it and utilise it to motivate ourselves to take incredible action each and every day.

Never take your eye off the prize, it's yours. It's your prize. Keep laser beam focus on your dreams and no obstacle can get in your way. No obstacle can stop you in your path. You are an unstoppable force of nature. Your why, your purpose, your mission is what motivates you to take massive action each and every single day to build unstoppable momentum and transform your dreams into a reality.

What do you dream of? What are your dreams? If you could do anything and knew you could not fail what would you do? Become an athlete of the mind and stop making excuses, stop blaming others, stop blaming your parents or your children or the economy or your environment. It's all you, you are responsible.

Step up and be a man, be a woman and take responsibility for your own life. No one can help you achieve your dreams but you, no one. Eliminate the word try, from your vocabulary, don't try, do. There is no try, only do or do not.

People say well I would like to get rich, I would like to travel the world, and I would like to meet my soul mate. What a weak word. Like, liking the idea of something never got us anywhere. We have to be hungry, thirsty, we have to crave it and want it so bad we cannot live without it. We must make our dreams come true as it is a part of our existence.

Kick but in the butt, but is a dream killer. Eliminate the word but as it negates anything said before it. People make excuses and blame others for their problems, you created all your own problems and only you have the power to solve them.

You have an untouched infinite reservoir of unlimited potential, unlimited power. The ability to harness this awesome power at any time is yours waiting right now to be unleashed upon the world.

Isn't it time you shined, and showed the world just how much greatness you have within you? And what you are really made of? Empower yourself now and begin with the first step by asking yourself what can I control, what can I do about this right now, what can I do right now to take one step closer to my dreams? Become an 'until' person. An 'until' person never quits EVER, period.

No matter what life throws at you, get back up, keep moving forward, keep growing and keep getting better. An 'until' person never quits on their family, on their friends, an 'until' person never quits on their dreams. They keep going no matter what until they are successful, until their dreams are a reality. Until!

An 'until' person works harder and does whatever it takes until they are successful. Get up as early as you need to, go to bed as late as you need to, what are you prepared to do to live a magnificent life many only dream of?

If it's not working then change your approach, change your

actions and reshape your path to get back on track to your destiny. Do whatever it takes in the relentless pursuit of your dreams. Stop procrastinating, stop wasting time. Today will never be here again and it could be your last.

You can do anything but you must do it now, and yes that includes achieving your dreams. Do you want to survive or do you want to thrive? Don't you want to thrive and live a life of freedom and abundance, of wealth and love?

One day you will die and it will be too late. So you've got to be hungry, you've got to create urgency in the attainment of your dreams. Dreams are like six pack abs, everyone wants them but only a few are prepared to do whatever it takes to have them!

Remember persistence beats resistance. Be strong no matter where you are, you can get anywhere if you stay focused on your dreams. Focused on your why. Mediocrity is not a comparison to anyone else. Mediocrity is when you settle for a life that's anything less than what you are capable of living and deserve. You deserve greatness. You deserve to live a momentous life. A grand life.

I dare you and I challenge you to think larger, expand your belief about what's possible. Expand your belief about what you can achieve.

There are two types of people in this world. People that die with regrets because they didn't take action, they made excuses, they pointed blame, they procrastinated and were afraid to make mistakes. And there are people that die happy because they did take action, they did live life to the max, they travelled the world, they played a bigger game, they loved, lived and learned and now they are ready to leave their legacy to their children that they can be proud of.

Who will you choose to be? Will you wait until it's too late, or will you commit right now? Will you decide to take massive action each and every day to achieve your dreams and help others do the same? Commit to excellence and be the best version of you, you can be. I dare you to raise the bar, give more and to live larger.

When was the last time you heard of someone on their deathbed saying, I wish I made more money, had more cars and homes?

Never. No one, ever. They wish they spent more time with their family, they wish they travelled more and contributed more. What are you doing to contribute to this beautiful world? How are you really making a difference?

At the end of the day all that really matters in life when we leave this world is two things: How you treated the people of this planet and how you treated Mother Earth. The question is, are you going to leave this world a better place for having been here?

Will you just go through life being content and living a mediocre life? Or will you create a life for you and your family with incredible magical memories and truly make a difference in this world?

Pain is temporary, regret is forever so take massive action and put the past behind you. Ditch that old excuse of a story. It's time to dream it, it's time to believe it, it's time to do it.

You've got to be ferocious in the pursuit of your dreams, you've got to be a lion in the jungle and walk tall, be proud, be confident, be majestic and walk the path you are destined to walk.

Everyone is going to die, until then play a bigger game, take risks, make mistakes, ask yourself the question, what can I do today to do more, be more and give more? The time will never be right, when is now a good time to act?

Waiting for the time to be right is like waiting to die, as every second that passes and is wasted is one second closer to the end, your end! You will feel fear, you will feel doubt, and you will be uncertain and unsure. Be courageous in the pursuit of your dreams, you deserve it. Feel the fear and do it anyway because you must, fear is only an illusion so are your dreams, you can choose to live your fear or you can choose to live your dreams

Which illusion will you feed and transform into your reality? What are you waiting for? Go now, get up, stand up, the time has come for you to put the past behind you, your time has come to be great, the time has come for you to be phenomenal. It's time for you to go out there and live your life and to live your dreams. With love and abundance.

Jason Grossman.

Act now. There is never any time but now, and there never will be any time but now.

—William Wattles

REFERENCES

American Speakers Bureau, 'Les Brown – Biography', viewed 16 February 2015 http://www.speakersbureau.com/speakers/brown/bio.htm

Biography Website, 'Mother Teresa – Biography', viewed February 16 2015 http://www.biography.com/people/mother-teresa-9504160

Biography Website, 'Nelson Mandela – Biography', viewed February 16 2015, http://www.biography.com/people/nelson-mandela-9397017

Biography Website, 'Richard Branson – Biography', viewed February 16 2015, http://www.biography.com/people/richard-branson-9224520

Christopher Gardner Media, 'Chris Gardner – Biography', viewed 16 February 2015, http://www.chrisgardnermedia.com/chris-gardner-biography.html

Covey, Dr Stephen R, 'The Big Rocks of Life', viewed February 16 2015, http://www.appleseeds.org/Big-Rocks_Covey.htm

Eker, T. Harv, http://www.success-guide.com/speakers/t-harv-eker/biography-t-harv-eker/

Ford, Henry, 'Henry Ford and the Assembly Line', viewed February 16 2015, http://history1900s.about.com/od/1910s/a/Ford--Assembly-Line.htm

Hendricks, Carla Adair, 2011, '86 Years of "I Do"', AARP Bulletin, viewed 16 February 2015, http://www.aarp.org/relationships/love-sex/info-08-2009/couple-maintains-world-record-for-longest-marriage.html

I.AM.ANGEL Foundation, viewed February 16 2015, http://iamangelfoundation.org/about/

Kamp, Karin, 2013, 'From Refugee Camp to Successful Entrepreneur', The Story Exchange, viewed 16 February 2015, http://thestoryexchange.org/role-model-stateless-refugee-immigrant-entrepreneur/

Kiyosaki, Robert, http://www.famous-entrepreneurs.com/robert-kiyosaki

Look to the Stars, 'Richard Branson – Charity Work, Events and Causes', viewed February 16 2015, https://www.looktothestars.org/celebrity/richard-branson

Sugars, Brad, http://www.actioncoach.com/meet-brad-sugars

The New Oprah, 'What Oprah Learned from Jim Carrey', viewed 16 February 2015, http://www.oprah.com/oprahs-lifeclass/What-Oprah-Learned-from-Jim-Carrey-Video